D0986744

KINGDOM
STEWARDSHIP

OCCASIONAL PAPERS PREPARED BY THE
LAUSANNE RESOURCE MOBILIZATION
WORKING GROUP FOR CAPE TOWN 2010

KINGDOM
STEWARDSHIP

OCCASIONAL PAPERS PREPARED BY THE
LAUSANNE RESOURCE MOBILIZATION
WORKING GROUP FOR CAPE TOWN 2010

Edited by
Arif Mohamed
Brett Elder
and Stephen Grabill

With a Foreword by Ram Gidoomal

Christian's LIBRARY PRESS

GRAND RAPIDS · MICHIGAN

Kingdom Stewardship
Occasional Papers Prepared by the Lausanne Resource
Mobilization Working Group for Cape Town 2010

Copyright © 2010

Reprinted 2011

Lausanne Committee for World Evangelization
www.lausanne.org

In encouraging the publication and study of these papers, the Lausanne Committee for World Evangelization does not necessarily endorse every viewpoint expressed in this book.

Cover image: Andrew Parfenov (04-17-07)
Giving
Source: istockphoto.com

All Scripture quotations, unless otherwise noted, are taken from the Holy Bible: New International Version (North American Edition). Copyright © 1973, 1978, 1984, by the International Bible Society. Used by permission of Christian's Library Press.

All rights reserved. No part of this publication may be reproduced, stored in a retrieval system, or transmitted in any form or by any means, including electronic, mechanical, photocopying, recording, or otherwise without the prior permission of the publisher.

ISBN 10: 1-880595-79-6
ISBN 13: 978-1-880595-79-4

Library of Congress Cataloging-in-Publication Data

CHRISTIAN'S LIBRARY PRESS
An imprint of the Acton Institute
for the Study of Religion & Liberty

161 Ottawa Avenue, NW, Suite 301
Grand Rapids, Michigan 49503
Phone: 616.454.3080
Fax: 616.454.9454
www.clpress.com

Cover design by Peter Ho
Interior composition by Judy Schafer

Printed by InnerWorking Inc., Grand Rapids, Michigan

830059

These occasional papers were prepared by the Resource Mobilization Working Group (RMWG) of the Lausanne Committee for World Evangelization to be used at the Lausanne Cape Town 2010 Conference.

The principal writers are Phill Butler, Dr. Sas Conradie, Dr. Terry Douglass, Brett A. Elder, Dr. Dion Forster, Ram Gidoomal, Dr. Stephen J. Grabill, Norris Hill, Kent Humphreys, Henry Kaestner, Rob Martin, Arif Mohamed, Paul Schultheis, and John C. Van Drunen.

This book was edited by Arif Mohamed, Brett Elder, and Stephen Grabill.

CONTENTS

FOREWORD

After the biennial Lausanne leaders meeting in Budapest, Hungary, in June 2007, Doug Birdsall, executive chairman of the Lausanne International Board of Directors, asked if my wife, Sunita, and I were prepared to meet two gentlemen who were having coffee at a sidewalk café nearby. We agreed and crossed the street to meet with Terry Douglass and Paul Schultheis and soon discovered why Doug had asked us to meet with them!

As we shared and exchanged our stories (over a few hours and several cups of coffee!) we discovered that, as individuals who had established and run successful businesses, we had all faced similar issues and challenges relating to our responsibilities for the finances with which we had been entrusted.

We had been stirred to ask similar questions, such as: What does the Bible teach about why we should give? How should we give? Where should we focus and target our giving? Were there needs that remained unfulfilled because of our lack of awareness and strategic thinking? Were we guilty of over-funding certain sectors or, alternatively, were the funds we were giving being used as effectively as possible? Were there others who were facing similar challenges and asking similar questions, and would there be strategic value in calling together like-minded individuals to discuss and pray through these issues in greater depth so we can learn from one another and share ideas and good practices?

The result was the formation of the newest Lausanne Working Group – the Resource Mobilization Working Group (RMWG). The RMWG held its first meeting in Washington, D.C., in February 2008 followed by three subsequent meetings at The National Christian Foundation offices in Atlanta. Meetings had also been held in South Africa and Nepal. Over one hundred participants were invited to these consultations to share and discuss a wide range of topics and issues relating to the stewardship dilemma – *why*, *how*, and *where* to give.

The result was *Kingdom Stewardship* – an edited collection of papers presented during the Washington and Atlanta consultations. While the key contributors have been identified, I want to acknowledge the helpful input of the many participants who attended the consultations. Their insights and critiques have helped to sharpen our thinking and to shape our *vision* of a global culture of generosity and effective stewardship of God's resources to support world evangelization and our *mission* to enable the discovery, development, and deployment of God's resources for world evangelization by catalyzing Global Generosity Networks in the twelve Lausanne regions.

I want to acknowledge the generous support of many individuals and foundations including Paul Schultheis of Strategy Resources Group (SRG); David Wills of The National Christian Foundation (NCF) who took on the chairmanship of the North American Resource Mobilization Working Group in 2009, Daryl Heald of The Maclellan Foundation, Fred Green of the Bolthouse Foundation, Terry Douglass of the ProVision Foundation, Kent Humphreys of Fellowship of Companies of

Christ International, Alan Barnhart of Barnhart Crane, Manfred Kohl of Overseas Council, Henry Kaestner of Ministry Spotlight, Chi Kong Shue, Santosh Shetty, and many others. The consultations would not have been possible without their generous support.

I am grateful for the administrative support given by Ron Ensminger and Terri Gibson (SRG) and Angela Smith (NCF). They played key roles in organizing the consultations and in following up speaker invitations, presentations, and papers. I also want to thank Ben Johnson (Maclellan Foundation) for his diligence in coordinating production of the RMWG Resource DVD for Cape Town 2010.

The efforts of the RMWG have been undergirded by prayer, and we are grateful to Beverley Pegues, co-founder and president of the Window International Network (WIN) who took on the responsibility to ensure that our work was and continues to be covered in prayer. We are grateful to her for mobilizing prayer support for our work as well as to Sarah Plummer of the Lausanne Prayer Working Group.

Members of other Lausanne Working Groups have also given helpful input to our work. In this regard, I want to thank Chris Wright (Theology), Jerry White (Business, Government, Education, Media, and Medicine), and Naomi Frizzell (Communications). The RMWG appreciates their generous investments of time and helpful feedback and critique of our work.

I also want to extend sincere appreciation to my colleagues on the International Resource Mobilization Working Group steering committee who have joined us on this journey, joyfully and willingly. They include Adel Azmy (Egypt/Lausanne Young Leaders Team), Andy Corley (UK), Daryl Heald (US), David Wills (US), Dennis Tongoi (Kenya), Dr. Dion Forster (South Africa), Edison Queiroz (Brazil), Ivor Poobalan (Sri Lanka), Jokebed Thierra (Mali), Rev. Fang Bing (China), Henry Kaestner (US), Joseph Steinberg (UK), Paul Schultheis

(US), Rob Martin (US), Santosh Shetty (Dubai/India), Terry Douglass (US), Zekai Tanyar (Turkey), Pastor Sofia Zhukotanskaya (Ukraine), and Dr. Wilson Agha (Nigeria).

Our editors Arif Mohamed, Brett Elder, and Stephen Grabill have done an excellent job in organizing a disparate and diverse set of papers to produce this professional publication on behalf of the RMWG – Thank you!

Ultimately, I am grateful to Dr. Sas Conradie of the CMS Mission Stewardship Department for his unstinting support and servant heart that has supported the work of the RMWG and helped coordinate our activities toward the Cape Town Congress and beyond!

We are all engaged in a journey that will – with your involvement and prayers – move the generosity dial to help fulfill the Great Commission of our Lord and Savior Jesus Christ: "Therefore go and make disciples of all nations" (Matt. 28:19-20).

– Ram Gidoomal CBE
Chairman, Lausanne Resource
Mobilization Working Group
Deputy Chairman,
Lausanne International
Board of Directors

Introduction

Brett Elder
Stephen Grabill

At the beginning of the twenty-first century, an unprecedented opportunity exists to disciple the church in the fundamental biblical pattern of holistic stewardship.

As the church becomes increasingly aware of issues of sustainability, seeks to understand and foster the role of business, and expands the message of the grace of giving as a central motif of the Christian life, an environment for personal and corporate transformation is beginning to take root.

Christ-centered stewardship – management of God's resources for his intended purposes – will begin to foster more accountability among businesses and ministries, more collaboration among ministry efforts for greater effectiveness, and healthy motivations and patterns of giving in the lives of all Christians, regardless of wealth, location, or status.

Abundant Generosity

The past fifty years have seen incredible successes in the worldwide church. We have experienced the growth of the house church movement in China and the spread of the gospel in

1

Africa. God has stirred the body of Christ to work in unity across the denominations for the sake of the gospel.

Imagine if the hearts of Christians around the world were recaptured by the self-giving example of Christ's love being poured out for us on the cross? What might that kind of radical Christian giving look like, reflected in the world today? How much more effectively would the church serve the world if our Christian unity translated into sustainable, collaborative ministry ventures?

God's priority is his church, not his resources. God gave everything for us, and when we give ourselves fully to him we become a more vivid reflection of his overwhelming abundance. God calls us to adjust our priorities and steward his resources for his ultimate purposes.

When we respond to God's abundant generosity and support kingdom causes freely, he blesses both parts of his body: the generators of wealth and funds and also the workers in the field. And in partnering, we discover the purpose God has planned for us.

The Kingdom Stewardship Papers

As a compilation of essays on stewardship and generosity themes from authors around the world, the chapters in this book offer a range of perspectives on issues that concern all in attendance at the Third Lausanne Congress on World Evangelization in Cape Town, South Africa.

The first chapter, "Kingdom Stewardship," gives an overview of what we mean by that term, explaining the *Who*, *What*, *How*, and *Why* of stewardship.

We then preface the discussion of possibilities and strategies with a few examples of kingdom work at its best. Ideally, stewardship and mission work in remote locations transforms communities into agents of transformation themselves. The story of Mizoram, India, in the second chapter, illustrates how effective stewardship can be "a gift that keeps on giving." Also in this chapter, we read the story of Graham Power, a businessman who, after seeing his success as a blessing from God, decided to mold his company into one that exists to serve God's kingdom. Finally, Terry Douglass shares how his service organization www.HaitiServe.org is giving lasting assistance to Haitians through resource mobilization rather than merely the donation of consumables.

Kent Humphreys, in the third chapter, "Engaging the Heart," uses Scripture to remind us that our responsibilities and desires to be God's stewards comes from a renewed heart; to keep our efforts honest and sincere, we must examine and strengthen that source first.

In chapter 4, "Strongholds," begins our exploration of obstacles to effective stewardship. Paul Schultheis outlines what are often the root causes of our problems – pride, fear, guilt, the hoarding impulse, and theological confusion – and John Van Drunen follows with an analysis of an issue that Christians often avoid addressing – ecclesiastical crime.

In chapter 5, "Survey, Research, and Action," brings *Kingdom Stewardship* to focus in our modern world – that is, global stewardship. With his story of a young man eager to share the gospel in a foreign country but lacking the funds to do so, Sas Conradie illustrates the need for cooperation and interconnectedness in the church's global mission work. He emphasizes that not only can global cooperation increase the flow of funds to places where they are most needed but that cooperation necessarily brings about smarter and more strategic multisectoral giving. The modern world, he writes, presents us with "an unprecedented opportunity for the global Christian community to collaborate and share resources more strategically and effectively with one another." This chapter closes with an incredibly detailed and convincing case for the global church to take advantage of the Internet, using modern technology as a tool, says Henry Kaestner, to transform the life of "recipient *and* giver."

In chapter 6, "Setting Standards," we get an honest look at the state of resource-sharing in the global Christian church today from three authors who agree on the need for greater unity, understanding, and more effective models for giving across borders. Rob Martin describes "the sometimes acrimonious and often confusing interactions between resources and missions" and gives us hope in a new program within the Lausanne movement called the Oxford Initiative. Phill Butler explains that if we hope to become more effective stewards and disciples, it means doing some serious research and analysis of practical models. What we need, Butler writes, are "strong, sustainable alternatives to the older, often dependency producing models." Finally, Henry Kaestner takes a look at the Christ-Centered Economic Development Initiative (CCED), again emphasizing the pursuit of dignity over dependency and explaining how the practical strategies and principles of CCED might be standardized.

When it comes to global stewardship, unity and effectiveness go together, as Norris Hill, Terry Douglass, and Henry Kaestner make clear in chapter 7, "Unity: Practicing Relational Stewardship." Hill opens the chapter with an eloquent discussion of relational stewardship. Douglass reminds us of the biblical call for unity in the body of Christ, the church. Kaestner writes that, through collaboration, we must seek to learn from the mistakes of one another and move toward clear and common ways of thinking about and of heeding our call to stewardship. Hill sums up the meaning behind relational stewardship and brings us to the basis of all Christian stewardship as he writes:

Therefore, to be a good steward is to let yourself be loved in a relationship with Christ and to let others be loved by Christ through your continued relationship with them. This is relational stewardship: a pursuit of God's unique vision and call on an individual's life through consistent Christ-centered relationship.

1

KINGDOM STEWARDSHIP

Ram Gidoomal

Christ-Centered Steward Discipleship

While most, if not all, Christians employ stewardship language to describe God's mission in the world, the foundational theological understanding of what stewardship is varies greatly across denominations and religious traditions.

Some groups think stewardship is tithing; others think stewardship means volunteering or living a simple lifestyle. Still others identify stewardship with environmental conservation, social action, charitable giving, or the making of disciples through evangelism.

Each of these good and necessary activities point to an essential facet of stewardship, but each, on its own, falls shy of capturing the inspiring vision of biblical stewardship as a form of whole-life discipleship that embraces every legitimate vocation and calling to fulfill God's mission in the world. In this sense, holistic stewardship, transformational generosity, workplace ministry, business as mission, and the theology of work movement all share a common point of origin in the biblical view of mission as whole-life discipleship.

However, this inspiring vision has suffered a setback in recent years. Why? It was set back for two primary reasons: (1) because evangelicals siphoned stewardship off from a holistic understanding of God's mission in order to raise funds for global missions and the local church; and (2) because evangelicals, at the same time, upheld the problematic distinction between clerical vocations and ordinary vocations, which only served to reinforce the age-old wall that had been erected between sacred and secular callings.

In the immediate aftermath of the First International Congress on World Evangelization, John Stott, in his 1975 Oxford lectures entitled *Christian Mission in the Modern World*, pinpointed the theological root cause of the problem. He discerned that evangelicals seemed unable to satisfactorily integrate the Great Commandment: "Love your neighbor as yourself" (Lev. 19:18) with the Great Commission: "Therefore go and make disciples of all nations" (Matt. 28:19).

God's mission, Stott urged in keeping with Matthew 5:13-16, "describes rather everything the church is sent into the world to do. [It] embraces the church's double vocation of service to be 'the salt of the earth' and 'the light of the world'" (pp. 30-31). The aim of the Lausanne movement is for the whole church to present the whole gospel to the whole world.

We, at the Resource Mobilization Working Group, believe that a proper understanding of the scope of God's mission places a stewardship responsibility on every Christian to join with the Son in the power of the Spirit to fulfill the Father's purpose in creation and redemption. At its most basic level, biblical stewardship is holistic and missional, touching every area of life and employing every legitimate vocation in service to Jesus Christ, "the firstborn over all creation" and "the head of ... the church" (Col. 1:15-20).

In light of this renewed sense of mission, the charge of the Committee is to offer the global church a robust concept of kingdom stewardship and generosity through the distribution of strategic biblical resources as well as advance a global opportunity to increase kingdom collaboration to support sustainable ministry worldwide through the use of today's emerging technologies and unprecedented connectivity.

Kingdom Stewardship

Stewardship is a central theme throughout Scripture much like the fundamental biblical themes of creation, fall, redemption, and consummation. Before we go much further, however, we need to come to a common understanding of the term.

The term *stewardship* has been a bit abused over the years. Webster defines *stewardship* as the "management of someone else's property." This may be an accurate enough definition for most uses, but the word *stewardship* is a translation of the Greek word *oikonomia* that primarily relates to the financial management of a household. The term is a combination of *oikos*, house, and *nomos*, law.

In classical Greek usage, the word had two meanings: (1) to exercise an administrative capacity; and (2) the office of the administrator or steward. It was used for such things as the arrangement of a building, the disposition of speech, and particularly, for the financial administration of a city.

In the gospels, *oikonomia* is used principally to mean the management or administration of the property of others (Matt. 20:8; Luke 12:42; and Luke 16:2). Matthew's account of the Parable of the Talents (25:14-30) and Luke's Parable of the Shrewd Manager (16:1-13) clearly illustrate this usage of *oikonomia*.

In Paul's letters, however, *oikonomia* is given its fullest and widest significance. It is applied (1) to the responsibility entrusted to Paul for preaching the gospel (1 Cor. 9:17);

9

(2) to the stewardship committed to Paul to fulfill the divine plan and purpose relative to the church that is the body of Christ (Eph. 3:2); and (3) to the arrangement or administration of God, which as the letter to the Ephesians states, was "set forth in Christ as a plan for the fullness of time, to unite all things in him, things in heaven and things on earth" (Eph. 1:9-10; 3:9; 1 Tim. 1:4).

The meaning here is that God is the Master of a great household (*cosmos*), and he is wisely administering his rule over it. He is doing this through the person of his son, Jesus Christ, who has in turn commissioned his human stewards (Gen. 1:28-30) to manage the Father's household through the animating power of the Holy Spirit.

At its core, biblical stewardship is a coronation of God's human stewards to fulfill the Father's mission in creation and redemption. This is a profound privilege and goes well beyond simply being a wise trustee of God's money and property. In fact, Scripture tells us that each of us is a steward of God's creation and design for every area of life.

Our management of God's resources is not a request; it is a fact. We do not choose to be managers of God's resources, God has already *entrusted* his resources to us. The following discussion of the *Who, What, How*, and *Why* of stewardship has been adapted and expanded at points from the Introduction to the *NIV Stewardship Study Bible*.

The *Who* of Stewardship

Everyone forms an understanding of what it means to be a steward – even an effective steward. In other words, almost everyone agrees that we need to be effective and responsible managers of money, time, resources, and opportunities. Whether we are talking about financial stewardship, environmental stewardship, or corporate stewardship, who would argue that we should not manage each of these areas effectively?

Yet, if we go back to the definition of stewardship (i.e., "the management of someone else's stuff"), we first need to determine the *Who* of stewardship. By definition, we are managing for someone else. However, for whom are we managing these arenas of life? Depending on whom you ask, you will get a variety of answers.

Scripture, however, tells us that we are managers of God's estate. We see already in Genesis 1 that God is the sole founder and owner of the cosmic enterprise we call the universe. Scripture leaves no doubt about his uncontested ownership and control of all he has made, from the earth itself to natural resources to plants and animals.

At no time in Scripture do we ever read about God relinquishing his ownership of anything he created. Psalm 24:1-2 reminds us, "The earth is the Lord's, and everything in it, the world, and all who live in it; for he founded it upon the seas and established it upon the waters." God's sovereign right to his creation is further reinforced by Psalm 50:10-12, "For every animal of the forest is mine, and the cattle on a thousand hills. I know every bird in the mountains, and the creatures of the field are mine. If I were hungry I would not tell you, for the world is mine, and all that is in it."

God is the *Who* of stewardship. We are managing for the living God. Other people or organizations may benefit along the way as we become effective stewards. However, our primary responsibility is to the One who entrusted all things into our care.

The *What* of Stewardship

Having established God as the Creator and owner of all that we see and experience, the next question is to ask: "*What* has God entrusted to our care?" The *NIV Stewardship Study Bible* reveals fourteen distinct areas of life that God has designed for us to steward. These areas reflect the *What* of stewardship.

As stewards, we can understand our divine commission as a "Manager in Trust."

This mnemonic device, though most helpful for English speaking audiences, is nonetheless an easy-to-remember framework of the roles and responsibilities of a biblical steward. Each letter represents a slice of life we have been called to steward.

Let us quickly run through it word-by-word and letter-by-letter.

M-A-N-A-G-E-R I-N T-R-U-S-T

The first word is **MANAGER**:

M – stands for God's **Mission** in the world
A – relates to **Absolute Truth**
N – represents our **New Life** in Christ
A – refers to tangible **Assets** of all sorts such as money and property
G – is for **Grace** (and the means by which it is administered, think here of communion, baptism, prayer, and so forth)
E – stands for the **Environment**
R – represents God's **Revelation** to his people

The second word is **IN**:

I – is for **Institutions** of all varieties
N – stands for our **Natural** bodies

The third word is **TRUST**:

T – is for **Time**
R – is for **Relationships**
U – refers to the development of our individually **Unique** character
S – stands for **Service** to others
T – is for **Talents** and natural abilities

God entrusts all these realms of responsibility to our careful management.

The *How* of Stewardship

The first major theme of stewardship recurring through-out Scripture is the fact that God is the author and owner of all things: seen and unseen. Closely associated with this overarching theme of God's ownership is the idea that our effective stewardship of all things must be evaluated by God's standards. In other words, since God is the Creator of this world, who better to ask about how to manage every arena of life effectively than the author and designer himself?

Stewardship and generosity are two of the Christian's most profound privileges. They are privileges granted by a God that loves us and wants only the best for each of us. God does not want us to view them as responsibilities to be performed or obligations placed on us by an uncaring God.

Imagine – the God of the universe has called you and me to be his stewards. This curious fact alone should move us to discover not only *what* has been entrusted to our care, but also *how* God intends every area of life to be managed for his ultimate glory.

We serve a perfect God – a God who does not have some vague idea of how life best functions. God's design for life is flawless. Since humanity fell into sin and became separated from God, our tendency is to manage life as if it were our own – as if we know what is best for us and how God's mission can best be accomplished.

We can only understand the *How* of stewardship when we seek to know and understand the *Who* of stewardship. Effec-tive stewardship can only be achieved when we diligently seek the One for whom we are commissioned as royal stewards.

The *Why* of Stewardship

Why would an all-knowing, all-powerful God, who is in control of all he created, appoint us as stewards over his resources?

God does not need us to be his stewards. God is more than capable of managing his creation. If God does not *need* us to be his stewards, why has he *chosen* us to be his stewards?

A close study of Scripture reveals seven purposes for why God has commissioned us as his stewards.

1. God wants his stewards to have **unquestionable character**. Our effective stewardship prompts us toward who we are called to be as individuals. We are God's image bearers. This is a profound privilege and responsibility. Such a responsibility requires a lifetime of intentional stewardship.

2. God seeks to develop in his stewards **undying commitment**. Our effective stewardship prompts us toward obedience to God regardless of the cost. God entrusts resources into our responsibility – money, assets, intelligence, time, freedom, institutions, relationships of all kinds, children, and the possessions that can sometimes clutter life. In return, he expects that our management of these things reflect our undying commitment to him.

3. God wants his stewards to exhibit **unwavering conformity** to his will as we become more conformed to his image. Our effective stewardship prompts us toward conforming to God's will and desires. It is only in our relentless and consistent pursuit of God that he reveals his good and perfect plan for our lives. His perfect will for our lives is far beyond what we can dream up on our own.

4. God desires his stewards to demonstrate **unquenchable compassion**. Our effective steward-

ship prompts us toward placing others' needs before our own. Throughout Scripture, we read of God's desire for us to be generous givers; to live life open-handedly. The apostle Paul tells us in 2 Corinthians 8:7 that God further desires us to "excel in the grace of giving." We were designed to live in relationship, in community with others. God desires that we share his heart for those he places in our path.

5. God has gifted each of his stewards with a **unique calling**. Our effective stewardship prompts us toward fulfilling our unique role in the body of Christ. God lovingly informs us in Psalm 139:13 that he has knit each one of us together in our mother's womb. We are individually unique creatures. As a species, we are unique among all of the creatures God brought into being.

6. God wants his stewards to have a sense of **unparalleled commission**. Our effective stewardship prompts us to recognize the privilege of sharing in the fulfillment of God's mission. As we seek to become effective stewards in every area of life, we become much better equipped to play a part, however small or large, in the unparalleled commission of sharing the Good News of Jesus Christ.

7. God wants his stewards to engage in **unending celebration** of his glory. Our effective stewardship prompts us to continually glorify the One who has chosen us to be his stewards. As we mature in our stewardship, our motivation for the management of his gifts increasingly reflects our desire to glorify, honor, and praise him simply because he is worthy of that expression.

Becoming Kingdom Stewards

God's purposes for stewardship may best be understood through the lens of his plan, his people, and his process:

Plan – God has entrusted us with his Son to repair our broken relationship with him. He entrusts us with a relationship with his Son. Our response is perhaps the greatest stewardship decision we will ever face.

People – An even greater secret is the fact that God has chosen us to implement his mission in the world. God could have chosen a multitude of other ways – including options that we cannot humanly conceive of – and yet he chose you and me to accomplish this urgent task. Think of it, God, knowing that we have a tendency to fail him on a regular basis, chose – and still chooses – us to spread the gospel and to make disciples of all nations.

Process – In his infinite wisdom, God has also entrusted his resources to us to accomplish the tasks he set before us. He provides us with everything we need to accomplish his divine purposes. He chooses to rely on us to share our resources. He chooses to rely on us to exercise our God-given vocations and callings to fulfill his mission in the world.

All of us have been entrusted with resources designed and created by God. Each of us has the opportunity to serve and glorify God with what he has entrusted to our care. Every individual is a steward by God's intention. However, God does not want us to manage his creation by *default*. He wants us to manage it by *design*: His design.

2

SPREADING THE MESSAGE: STORIES AND CASE STUDIES

THE STORY OF MIZORAM

Arif Mohamed

Mizoram, North India, is an example of a whole community being transformed through the gospel and, in turn, resourcing their region and other nations. This vibrant and adventurous Christian society has a strong belief in evangelism and mission. Consequently, it sends out proportionately more missionaries than any other community in the world.

This was not always the case with Mizoram. As recently as the 1950s, it was an incredibly poor region, animistic in its beliefs. Since then, it has changed beyond recognition, and 86 percent of Mizos now follow Jesus.

Mr. Lalchuangliana is a man who grew up in the village of Aizawl, the capital of Mizoram. In many ways, he embodies the spirit of Mizoram, which has produced innumerable leaders from its community of around 800,000 people.

He has worked in missions since 1973. Between 1973 and 1996, he headed the Emmanuel Hospital Association, a group of 20 hospitals and community health projects, serving half a million people a year with 50,000 operations. He also designed a unique system of federal cooperative societies, and now leads a team of 52 organizations that plant churches in various parts of North India. They currently have 37,000 churches throughout the region.

"Mizoram is a unique transformational story," says Lalchuangliana. "I come from a small, tribal community which, by the grace of God, has been wonderfully transformed. And I am a beneficiary of that transformation."

The First Church

Mizoram's Christian story begins in the 1890s, when the first church and mission headquarters were established. The tombstones of the first two Mizo Christians, who died in 1905, can still be seen in Aizawl.

Mizoram's spiritual transformation can best be seen in the way it has physically changed over a short period of time. The original church building has been torn down, rebuilt, and expanded several times. The community is currently constructing a huge, four-story building, costing about five crores (50 million rupees, which is roughly US$1.1m).

Meanwhile, the Mizoram Christians have experienced unprecedented blessings. In 1948, the first high schools in Mizoram were established. This began a wave of education resulting in a college being built in 1970, outgrown, and replaced with a larger one, which now offers BD and BTh courses.

A third of Mizos are in schools, colleges, and universities, with about 10,000 Mizo students in establishments in different parts of India.

Mizoram now has libraries, banks, and cooperative societies where before there was nothing. One woman started a highly successful bakery that provided the resources to rebuild her house into a sizable home for her family.

Aizawl also has its own small airport. "Twenty-five years ago, three-quarters of the people of Mizoram said that an airport will never be built in Mizoram and an aircraft will never land in Mizoram," says Lalchuangliana. The village also generated the resources to completely redevelop the winding dirt track into town, traveled by Pandit Nehru and Indira Gandhi when they visited Mizoram in 1953.

Evidences of Transformation

"We see evidences of transformation everywhere, as people live in better houses and enjoy a higher standard of living and education, as well as better health, longevity, and peace in the community," said Lalchuangliana.

There is no doubt among the community that its material success is due to the blessing of God. Praise and prayer are a way of life for Mizos. There are big churches all over Mizoram for denominations that include Presbyterian and Baptist, though the community acts as one body, regardless of denominations. In fact, it sends out about two thousand missionaries a year to different parts of India, as well as Samoa, China, Thailand, and even England. "Wherever we are, we start and lead churches, for example in Delhi," says Lalchuangliana. He says that Mizo people feel a responsibility to sow generously into missions, because of the blessing they have received.

Mizoram's investment in missions has grown exponentially over the years, from just 26 Rupees in 1932; Rs.758 in 1952; Rs.21 million in 1982; to over Rs.20 billion in 2007 (around $US447 million). "We thank God there is an example of a whole community being transformed through the gospel, and we feel truly blessed," comments Lalchuangliana.

RESOURCE MOBILIZATION IN CAPE TOWN

Dion Forster

Graham Power is the founder and owner of the Power Group of Companies, the largest privately owned construction, property development, and civil engineering business in South Africa. It employs 1500 staff and is a significant contributor toward the development of infrastructure in South Africa such as highway construction, schools, hospitals, power stations, and affordable housing.

Graham started his business with one small pickup truck and his wife as his only employee in 1983. Through drive and determination, the Power Group grew to its current size, under the blessing of God. Consequently, Graham's success story is a great illustration of what happens when business people dedicate and mobilize resources for the sake of God's kingdom.

Small Choices with Big Results

Graham moved from being a nominal Christian to a confessing one in February 1999. He had grown up in humble circumstances and started out in the construction industry in a very basic position. Graham quickly rose through the ranks of the company and in 1983 started his own business, now the highly successful Power Group. However, in spite of this success and wealth, he lacked peace.

Graham found the Lord after attending two Christian business breakfast events, which led him to dedicate his whole life, family, and business to God – twenty-four hours a day, seven days a week.

In 2001, Graham became the visionary leader for a gathering in Cape Town that saw 45,000 Christians fill Newlands Stadium to pray for the needs of the nation. Today, this movement has become the Global Day of Prayer. Meanwhile, his business has flourished.

Graham's testimony is a remarkable witness to many other Christians in business. What was significant about his conversion is the realization, from the very start, that Jesus wanted to be Lord of every part of his life, not just his spiritual life or church life. God has a will for his family and his business, and this would need to be discovered and obeyed.

Soon after Graham's conversion, he was invited to join a cell group with some other Christians and business peers. Graham had also drawn close to marketplace ministry leader, Adolph Schultz. Through these interactions, he started asking some questions: What is the purpose of work? Does God want to use my skills, influence, network of relationships, and wealth for a particular aim? What does God want to do with the Power Group? How much personal wealth is enough?

Bold Decisions

Through much soul searching and interaction, Graham came to make three very bold decisions:

First, the Power Group of companies would tithe on its profits. This would be channeled into a charitable trust that would allocate funds toward significant projects that would transform the lives of people in tangible ways, such as HIV/AIDS prevention and care, food security, economic empowerment, social development, and the protection of women and children.

Second, Graham capped his personal wealth. Other than his personal tithe, he also allocated the majority of his personal wealth and income into a second charitable trust, specifically aimed at the ministry and social transformation projects closest to his heart, such as the youth development center Eagles Rising, the Global Day of Prayer, and the Unashamedly Ethical campaign.

Third, the Power Group would adopt a strict code of values and ethics (which later contributed toward the formation of Unashamedly Ethical) in dealing with clients and employees. Many doubted that the company could continue to exist in a climate where price fixing, bribery, and false pricing were the norm. However, the Power Group has not only survived, it has shown remarkable growth and resilience as a result of its values, ethics, and clean living.

Stewardship Lessons

There are a number of lessons that can be learned from Graham Power and the Power Group relating to Christian stewardship and resource mobilization.

The first important lesson to learn is that God desires to have every part of one's life submitted to his will and purpose. This includes one's business life, one's business decisions, and of course one's wealth and influence. Graham is a very humble man whom God has been able to use to transform many social and political structures in South Africa, and particularly in the construction industry, because of his willingness to submit his whole life to the Lordship of Christ.

Second, we can learn from Graham that God has an intention and desire to use individuals and companies that have specific gifts and abilities in order to achieve the purposes of God's kingdom.

Third, through Graham's personal giving, and the giving from the profits of the company, he has learned that financial resources can make a significant difference in the lives of people and in furthering the kingdom of God, when carefully and strategically administered and invested.

The Power trusts have been intentional about allocating the majority of its available funds to larger projects that have a proven impact on society, and have shown themselves to be transformative and sustainable. Many Christians make the mistake of not investing their tithes and offerings wisely. We should seek to invest money in projects and ministries that are most likely to yield the greatest possible return for God's kingdom, whether they are explicitly Christian or not. The end result is to seek to leverage the available funds for the greatest benefit to God's desire to heal and restore individuals and society.

MAKING A DIFFERENCE IN HAITI

Arif Mohamed

The devastating earthquake in Haiti on Tuesday, January 12, 2010, saw hundreds of missions and relief organizations mobilize resources to aid the thousands of people in need.

HaitiServe, Inc., is one of the many excellent resource mobilizing initiatives that sprang into action, with the aim of "serving those who serve." HaitiServe is a nonprofit corporation formed to turn the earthquake disaster into an opportunity to transform Haiti and serve the Haitian people.

Dr. Terry Douglass of the ProVision Foundation was on the ground in Haiti shortly after the earthquake, working on the relief effort. Norris Hill led the team, which grew in numbers over the next few weeks, working together with the churches in Haiti to serve their communities.

Douglass says that HaitiServe's vision is "to see the people and nation of Haiti and those serving Haiti physically and spiritually transformed." Its mission, rooted in the gospel, is "to love and serve the people of Haiti with all of our heart, soul, mind, body, and spirit."

Community of Service Organizations

As Douglass explains, HaitiServe is a community of Haiti service organizations. It seeks to assist people in serving

23

their Haitian neighbors and to enable American and foreign churches to serve the churches of Haiti. Initial projects involved strengthening and rebuilding churches and supplying resources to help churches provide clinics, schools, orphanages, trade schools, and so on, to their communities. The organization identified leadership in about twenty-five churches and communities that needed help in church and community relief, restoration, rebuilding, and transformation, and which had both transformational and sustainable Haitian leadership.

In addition to assisting churches, HaitiServe was set up to help health care providers serve their counterparts in Haiti and similarly to assist businesses in serving the businesses of Haiti. It also aims to enable schools to serve the schools of Haiti, NGOs to serve the NGOs of Haiti, and governments to serve the government of Haiti, all of which ultimately serve the Haitians.

The ambitious initiative ensures that all projects are developed and operated in partnership with Haitian leadership, and that they will seek to be transformational.

HaitiServe supports a number of ministries, coordinating their activities and contributions. These include ProVision Foundation (www.provisionfoundation.org); Equitas Group (www.equitasgroup.org); Harvest Field (www.harvestfield-haiti.org); Chadasha Foundation and the Jimani Project (www.chadasha.org); Ubuntu, Cedar Springs Presbyterian Church (www.cspc.net); and The University of Tennessee Medical Center at Knoxville.

Mobilizing Human Resources

I spoke to Terry Douglass two months after the earthquake and he said, "We continue to send teams of eight volunteers to Haiti each week to our fixed site and field clinics there. We have added staff to serve in volunteer recruitment and coordination, orphanages and adoptions, construction, healthcare, and major projects." The organization also had two families serving in Haiti full-time and two houses for volunteers in Port-au-Prince.

As you can imagine, there are many great stories that have come from the HaitiServe initiative. Here is just one: "We were able to get a trailer load of food that was donated from the MiddleEast, supposedly by a Saudi prince, to be distributed to over 2,000 families through a Baptist Church we serve in Haiti," says Douglass.

He is hopeful that other types of resource mobilization programs will be generated through the work of HaitiServe, including business and microfinancing initiatives. "We are hiring Haitians as much as possible. We have discussed the possibility of setting up businesses to produce rehab appliances and to do construction."

The work of HaitiServe is ongoing, but Terry summed it up by saying, "Our general objective is to mobilize resources – time, talent, and treasure; people, churches, healthcare providers, businesses, schools, NGOs, and government – to serve the leadership of Haiti who are serving the people of Haiti with a common goal of spiritual and physical transformation."

3

ENGAGING THE HEART

Kent Humphreys

It Starts with the Heart

"I the Lord search the heart and examine the mind, to reward a man according to his conduct" (Jer. 17:10).

The basic problem behind providing proper resources for the worldwide church is not money, or processes, or organizations, or strategy but how we think. The basis of that is our hearts.

The passage 1 John 2:15-17 says:

> Love not the world, neither the things that are in the world. If any man loves the world, the love of the Father is not in him. For all that is in the world, the lust of the flesh, and the lust of the eyes, and the pride of life is not of the Father, but is of the world. And the world passes away.

There are three issues here: (1) the lust of the flesh or the desire to indulge; (2) the lust of the eyes or the desire to possess; and (3) the pride of life: the desire to impress. Each of us struggles in all three areas, but usually one of these areas is more difficult for us.

Our heart is to be focused on God, as we are to love Jesus Christ and not this world (Matt. 6:19-34). Furthermore, God says that for us to seek riches, honor, or a fulfilling life is sin; but if we seek him, then he will give to us riches, honor, and life (Prov. 22:4).

The Bible gives us the example of Solomon, in 1 Kings 3:8-14, who did not ask for a long life or wealth, but instead for wisdom. God gave to Solomon what he requested and added to it riches and honor. This is because God is concerned about the focus of our hearts.

The problem is: "The heart is deceitful above all things" (Jer. 17:9). Our hearts are in such bad shape that God has to give us a heart transplant. He continually – each day – gives us new hearts as we place our focus upon him (Ezek. 36:26, 27).

You may ask how evil things can come out of your heart since you want to seek God and live a good life. However, look at the life of David: If David was capable of adultery and murder, even though he was a "man after God's own heart," then it can happen to any of us at any time!

Meditating on this subject in the middle of the night, the Spirit of God asked me, "Kent, do you have a heart for serving God?" I answered, "Yes, Lord." Then he asked me, "Or, do you have a heart for God himself?" So much of the time my heart is focused on doing things "for God" instead of giving myself totally to God. How about you?

Scripture tells us that a heart for God is a heart that is broken, sincere and humble, pure and blameless; one that desires to know God; one of integrity; one that trusts him and is on the right path, fully committed to him.

A Renewed Heart

"I will give them an undivided heart and put a new spirit in them; I will remove from them their heart of stone and give them a heart of flesh" (Ezek. 11:19).

God allows us to make choices. We can seek the good, the bad, or his best for our lives. He allows us to make this choice many times each day (Job 22:22-26; Ps. 37:4-5). How can we personally focus on the very best that God has for us, and encourage others to do the same?

We must ask ourselves these questions: What is the focus of my heart? What am I doing daily to get it corrected? Do I realize that my basic problem is not organizational, or educational, but a heart issue? Do we as organizations realize that all scriptural giving stems from the heart?

Are we teaching this message to our young leaders? Are we appealing to the donor's pride and emotions, intellect and logic, or to the heart?

Are we looking at the donor's capacity and appearance, or to the heart? Are we using the world's methods of fund-raising, or are we appealing to the heart of a true follower of Christ?

If God captures the heart, then the wallet will follow!

Spiritual Pride

The Bible instructs us to know Christ (Phil. 3:10), to abide in him (John 15:5), to worship him (Col. 1:15-17), and to seek his kingdom (Matt. 6:33). However, spiritual pride can be a real danger when it comes to giving the Lord a sincere sacrifice through giving.

The Lord says: "Cursed is the one who trusts in man, who depends on flesh for his strength and whose heart turns away from the Lord ... But blessed is the man who trusts in the Lord, whose confidence is in him" (Jer. 17:5, 7).

29

In the Gospels, Jesus often warns against proud religious leaders:

> Beware of the teachers of the law. They like to walk around in flowing robes and love to be greeted in the marketplaces and have the most important seats in the synagogues and the places of honor at banquets. They devour widows' houses and for a show make lengthy prayers. Such men will be punished most severely.

Could there be a parallel with the front tables at our Christian conferences, or the best parking places in the car lot?

Hypocrisy is another danger that can prevent us from giving God our best. Luke 12:1-3 says:

> He began saying to his disciples first of all, "Beware of the leaven of the Pharisees, which is hypocrisy. But there is nothing covered up that will not be revealed, and hidden that will not be known. Accordingly, whatever you have said in the dark will be heard in the light, and what you have whispered in the inner rooms will be proclaimed upon the housetops."

Leaven is hypocrisy, the opposite of sincerity and truth. Wherever you have spiritual pride, you will have false teaching, and wherever you have false teaching, there you will have spiritual pride.

Prideful and public giving is the third danger. "Beware of practicing your righteousness before men to be noticed by them; otherwise you have no reward with your Father who is in heaven" (Matt. 6:1-4).

We must also beware of false prophets (Matt. 7:15-20) and false teaching (Matt. 16:6, 7 and Mark 8:15). These can create a "religious class system," resulting in a separation between the clergy and laity, or the professional and the ordinary. It can create a false division between those who have resources and those who need resources.

In conclusion, the problem with spiritual pride and hypocrisy is that they lead us to wrong thinking. The problem is not Satan or his demons, but us. We are modeling the very thing that Christ told us to beware.

Do It Now!

This world is passing away, and Jesus may come before we die. We are stewards of our time, talents, and resources, and we will be rewarded accordingly. Scripture is abundantly clear on this, as the following verse illustrates: "For the Son of Man is going to come in his Father's glory with his angels, and then he will reward each person according to what he has done" (Matt. 16:27).

In light of these passages, we might like to reflect on a few questions. What specifically is God asking you to do right now, this year? What is your heart's passion? What do you think about when the urgent is not controlling your thinking? What is the Holy Spirit giving you a sense of urgency about?

I recently learned the right question to ask business leaders as I travel overseas: "Would you allow me to walk with you and learn from you?" I do this to fight back my prideful impulse to act like I have something to offer that they need. Ministry need not be its own activity. I must simply model Christ and serve those whom God places in my path each day.

As to the question, "What must I do this year?" God first touches our heart, the source of all the troubles and inspirations of our lives. Then we consider these things with our mind. Finally, we act on what our heart is focused on and our mind is thinking about. When Jesus calls us to act, we must instantly obey. "Be very careful, then, how you live – not as unwise but as wise, making the most of every opportunity, because the days are evil. Therefore do not be foolish, but understand what the Lord's will is" (Eph. 5:15-17).

Reflective Exercise: Engaging the Heart

As stewards of the living God, we must constantly ask ourselves these questions.

> What is my life goal, and what is the passion of my life?
>
> In what area must I be careful this year to choose the best and not just the good?
>
> What lesson is God teaching me at this time?
>
> What is God asking me to do this year?
>
> What is the focus of my heart? Is it on Jesus Christ?
>
> What am I thinking about? Am I prideful or humble before my God?
>
> What has God asked me to do? When will I start?

Ten Principles for Giving as a Biblical Steward

God owns everything and does not need our money. He is trying to raise responsible children and wants us to learn to be profitable and effective stewards. Following are ten principles for giving as a biblical steward.

1. We are to give regularly and proportionately (1 Cor. 16:2).

2. We should not give out of fear or human effort to keep the law. For example, did you know that the three tithes in the Old Testament added up to 23 percent annually, not 10 percent? (Num. 18; Deut. 12, 14; Mal. 3:10).

3. We should give voluntarily out of love and gratitude to God (2 Cor. 8:3, 8).

4. We should give out of gratitude for what God has done in Christ and not to justify ourselves. God

will judge our hearts and motives! (Prov. 23:7; Luke 18).

5. We should give cheerfully (2 Cor. 8:7; 9:7); generously (Luke 6:38; 2 Cor. 9:6; 1 Tim. 6:18); secretly without ostentation (Matt. 6:3, 4); and sacrificially (Matt. 12:42).

6. We should give to the poor, orphans, widows, aliens (Deut. 14:28, 29) and to those who have helped us spiritually (Matt. 10:10; Gal. 6:6).

7. We should give to those who are humble servants of Christ (1 Cor. 3:3; 2 Cor. 1:12).

8. We should give to others in the body of Christ experiencing hard times (Acts 11:29; 1 Cor. 16:1; 2 Cor. 8:13, 14).

9. We should give where the investment will produce the best spiritual return.

10. We should give to those parts of the world that have never heard the gospel (Matt. 28:19, 20).

4

DISMANTLING STRONGHOLDS

CHALLENGES TO GENEROUS AND EFFECTIVE STEWARDSHIP

Paul Schultheis

Effective Stewardship

The central goal of resource mobilization is the wise deployment and effective stewardship of limited resources for greater kingdom impact. However, many things prevent individuals and groups of people from reaching their potential in giving; these can be considered "strongholds"

The Greek word for *stronghold* means "a fortress," but it is also used in Scripture as a metaphor for that which is based on human confidence or pride instead of God's input and guidance.

The apostle Paul uses the term *strongholds* in 2 Corinthians 10:4: "For the weapons of our warfare are not carnal, but mighty through God to the pulling down of strongholds."

In verse 5, Paul goes on to elaborate on what he means by strongholds: "casting down imaginations, and every high thing that is exalted against the knowledge of God, and bringing every thought into captivity to the obedience of Christ."

Many consider strongholds to be areas where there is demonic influence, rather than godly influence. Our intention here is not to discuss the extent to which strongholds may refer to demonic activity. Suffice it to say that Paul is very clear that strongholds oppose God and his plans, rather than generating obedience to him, and must therefore be challenged.

With this in mind, what are some of the strongholds that Christians face as they aim to be effective stewards? A non-exhaustive list includes pride, fear, guilt, lack of prayer, hoarding and warehousing, and theological errors, as we shall now discuss.

Stronghold of Pride

Pride in giving takes many forms and can present a barrier to effective stewardship. A good text to keep in mind is Matthew 6:1-4:

> Be careful not to do your "acts of righteousness" before men, to be seen by them. If you do, you will have no reward from your Father in heaven. So when you give to the needy, do not announce it with trumpets, as the hypocrites do in the synagogues and on the streets, to be honored by men. I tell you the truth, they have received their reward in full. But when you give to the needy, do not let your left hand know what your right hand is doing, so that your giving may be in secret. Then your Father, who sees what is done in secret, will reward you.

Pride can encompass independence in giving: going it alone rather than collaborating with others or providing joint funding. Pride allows the glory to go to the individual and says, "Look at me, I am the provider!"

Pride could also lead to "passion-driven" giving that makes the donor feel good or experience joy. Although there is no harm in enjoying being a generous giver, if we are doing this to feel better about ourselves, then we might need to re-examine our motives.

Alternatively, if the donor is giving resources to control the outcome or promote their own agenda, there is pride in this approach. Those who have money and resources may put themselves in a position of power over those who do not have, and this is obviously not godly. Arrogance in giving is always a danger; donors must never cease checking their heart response.

Fear and Guilt

For many, fear and guilt are huge strongholds in their lives, standing in the way of both generous giving and reaping the blessings of a bountiful God.

Luke 12:22 and 12:31 state: "Then Jesus said to his disciples: 'Therefore I tell you, do not worry about your life, what you will eat; or about your body, what you will wear... But seek his kingdom, and these things will be given to you as well.'"

Christians across the globe share a common fear of not being able to pay their taxes and bills. We face a fear of going broke and being poor, and this is the case even for those who have substantial wealth.

Fear of not having enough is an issue faced by whole organizations as well as individuals. As with fear of all types, the best way to combat it is with faith in God.

It is the same with guilt. We have a God of grace and love, who has freed us to live guilt-free lives (Gal. 5:1). Donors need to understand the radical truth that they are under no obligation to give. Consequently, they do not need to feel guilty if they do not give as they feel they should.

However, if they are convicted by the Holy Spirit to give, then this is a different matter. God wants us to give in response to the freedom we have. Given the opportunity to give, we can take part in the adventure of sharing resources with those who lack them! God wants liberated givers who are full of faith in him and are not guilt-ridden.

The issue of money can present other problems. In our churches, teachers and pastors and ministry leaders can be intimidated by money, and they either avoid preaching on it, or teach an antimoney message. "It is easier for a camel to go through the eye of a needle than for a rich man to enter the kingdom of God" (Mark 10:25).

In some quarters, a prosperity gospel may be preached, but in others there is an opposite message, a sort of negative prosperity gospel teaching. As a result, diligent stewards fear making mistakes and face "giving paralysis."

The solution here is for churches to teach well on money, wealth, and giving with a God-centered, kingdom-centered theology focused on the grace of God.

Lack of Prayer

Lack of prayer can also become a stronghold, preventing us from walking in God's will for us to be generous givers. James 4:2 says, "You do not have because you do not ask God." The Lord wants to provide, but lack of prayer can act as a barrier.

We are in danger of not praying enough for mobilization initiatives; offering no intentional intercessory prayer for those with financial stewardship responsibility, and no prayer as part of the granting process. In all of these things, more prayer would be very beneficial – if not essential.

Hoarding and Warehousing

There is a great temptation to conform to the world's values and habits of hoarding and warehousing resources. We can be tempted to hold onto wealth as insurance for tomorrow's difficulties.

Luke 12:15-21 warns against this in the parable of the rich man: "You fool! This very night your life will be demanded from you. Then who will get what you have prepared for yourself? This is how it will be with anyone who stores up things for himself but is not rich toward God."

Our battle is against conforming to worldly patterns and the accumulation and preservation of wealth. A sign of hoarding and warehousing is giving the minimum legal requirement, regardless of our actual earnings, the need, or the urgency.

By holding onto a "give the fruit but grow the orchard" model, we may be creating "good" warehouses, but we could also be hindering the supernatural provision of God.

Foundations, retirement funds, investment portfolios, insurance cash values, and long-term investment can aid the kingdom, but they can also trick us into tying up our "self worth" in our "net worth."

Again, good teaching from the churches will help to combat a mindset that is based on the values and concerns of this world. Pastors, teachers, and leaders at all levels have a role and responsibility to challenge the desire to hoard as the opposite of a desire to give.

Theological Issues

Theological issues can become strongholds that need to be challenged and overthrown. Matthew 16:18 says, "I will build my church and the gates of Hell will not prevail against it"; we have God's assurance in this.

However, confused theology can stagger resource-effective stewardship. We need to remember that God is sovereign and he will provide to those in need in his own time. All we must do is pray and act with faith.

Differences over evangelism can also cause problems. We are called to give and spread the gospel, to meet needs while evangelizing for the sake of the kingdom. However, disagreement on approaches to evangelizing can confuse givers and limit their generosity.

Other theological issues that can hinder effective stewardship include a lack of theological leadership or of a coherent worldview, and an emphasis on almsgiving rather than investing in the kingdom.

There may also be a disconnect between the secular and the sacred in church teaching, allowing Christians to forget that their whole lives, their church and nonchurch-related activities, come under the remit of Christ.

Finally, a lack of biblical teaching on planning and financial accountability and reporting can lead to believers that are theologically ill-equipped to be effective stewards.

Solutions

We have discussed strongholds of pride, fear, warehousing, and lack of prayer, which can act as barriers to effective giving. To conclude, here are some practical solutions that could help the church as a whole to improve in its role as God's steward.

- Apply Luke 12:22 and 12:31 corporately – mobilize prayer for financial stewards, as well as mobilization initiatives and the granting process itself.

- Teach well in churches to combat strongholds such as pride in giving, fear of giving, storing up resources, guilt, and lack of prayer.

- Establish a process for the development of theologically sound, biblically based best practices with endorsements by ministry and resource entities.

- Become financial partners with ministries, rather than donors and receivers, which can lead to dependency on donors.

Conduct an evaluation of the giving process, and the relationships at each link in the giving chain, because this will help to develop your stewardship strategy.

REDUCING ECCLESIASTICAL CRIME

John C. Van Drunen

Ecclesiastical crime is a huge problem for missions funding because it prevents much needed resources from reaching those who need it most and hinders kingdom work.

Black's Law Dictionary defines ecclesiastical crime as "The fraudulent taking of personal property with which one has been entrusted, especially as a fiduciary." The *International Bulletin of Missionary Research* describes ecclesiastical crime as "amounts embezzled by top custodians of Christian monies."

The fraudulent misuse of kingdom assets is done knowingly and recklessly by individuals, and although embezzlement is going to be the largest part of this, the problem is likely to be far bigger, which is a cause for concern. As stewards of kingdom resources, we must all be above reproach (1 Tim. 3), recognizing that we are stewards, not owners (Luke 19:13), and that faithfulness is required of those entrusted (1 Cor. 4:2).

Getting on top of ecclesiastical crime will help us to protect kingdom resources, hold brothers and sisters in Christ accountable and reduce the risk of diminishing our organizations' Christian witness.

The question is: How do we go about measuring the problem? Is the amount of money stolen each year $27 billion or $27 million? We do not currently have the answer, and, in fact, reports from the Association of Certified Fraud Examiners (ACFE) and the *International Bulletin of Missionary Research* have indicated that it is difficult to quantify the universe of ecclesiastical crime.

In a 2008 report, the ACFE identified what it terms "primary internal control weaknesses" in Christian organizations. Much of the crime happens because of a lack of internal controls (in 37 percent of organizations), lack of management review of controls (19 percent) and the overriding of existing controls (19 percent).

Other problems include (1) leaders not setting the right tone for financial stewardship; (2) lack of competent oversight; (3) lack of independent checks and audits; and (4) lack of clear lines of authority.

The ACFE is also helpful in pointing out the behavioral red flags that exist in people who are involved in fraud schemes, which could be useful in helping to identify those prone to or engaged in ecclesiastical crime, though wisdom is obviously called for in acting on any suspicions.

For example, the individual may have a "wheeler-dealer attitude," face excessive pressure from within the organization or at home, or be living beyond their means. They may have control issues, and an unwillingness to share duties. Other signs may include refusal to take vacations, addiction problems, past legal problems, irritability, suspiciousness or defensiveness. They may have past employment-related problems, complain about inadequate pay or lack of authority, have family problems or other instability issues, or be facing financial difficulties (Source: ACFE 2008 Report to the Nation on Occupational Fraud and Abuse).

While knowing the warning signs can be helpful, is measurement practical? For starters, this sort of crime is extremely difficult to gauge accurately because there is a problem with knowing what to measure, and what to use as the control.

Establishing Better Practices

Rather than trying to measure the problem, a more effective approach is fraud education and the promotion of better practices.

First, we need to accept that Christian organizations are susceptible to financial crime. We often display the Ostrich Syndrome, sticking our heads in the sand, and working in an environment of blind trust, saying, "We're all Christians working to further the kingdom," and, "We don't have the resources to implement internal controls." We focus on program activities to the detriment of being accountable in our processes.

We also need to recognize that fraud will happen as long as there is sin. We therefore need to adopt a risk assessment model to protect our organizations from fraud. This might include demanding Christian peer accountability, encouraging responsible and prudent practices, and getting the news out that our organizations are not immune to fraud. In fact, Christian organizations may be more susceptible to fraud than has been previously thought.

We may also need to be more proactive in dealing with our financial resources. Establishing independent boards can set the right tone at the top, as will having independent financial or audit committees.

Other steps that can help are: setting or strengthening internal control procedures, ensuring management review takes place, revising or enhancing procedures, having conflicts of interest policies and procedures, and setting up a fraud or whistleblower policy or hotline.

Finally, evangelical organizations might consider ECFA membership, which allows organizations to step up and take a stand for integrity. Members benefit from "field review" processes that allow accountability to remain fresh with organizations and their staff. Also, ECFA's Compliance Program offers a venue for complaints to be addressed by an independent third-party, bringing a greater level of assurance.

5

SURVEY, RESEARCH, AND ACTION

GLOBAL STEWARDSHIP IN THE TWENTY-FIRST CENTURY

Sas Conradie

Realities of a Global World

I grew up in a conservative Afrikaner community in apartheid South Africa in the 1970s when the divide between rich white and poor black communities was profound. Contact between people from different cultures was nearly nonexistent and actually illegal.

In the mid 1980s, I became involved in mobilizing South African students for mission work; not only the privileged white students, but also African students who had a call for mission but who came from extreme poverty.

The challenge hit home in 1992 when an African student came to me after I provoked students to engage in world evangelization. This student had a clear calling to go as a missionary to the former Soviet Union.

Having a real passion for bringing people to Christ, he had been praying for Russia for a number of years and had already been involved in evangelism. In my mind, he was a much better mission candidate than many of the white students who were more interested in adventure than in the opportunity for evangelism.

The problem was that this student came from a church of one hundred people in one of the poorest communities in South Africa. Unfortunately, mission agencies required the equivalent of at least $2,000 to $3,000 a month before somebody could go through their agency to Russia. That amount was totally unaffordable to this student.

I began looking for ways to help him and called one of the mission mobilization leaders in South Africa. His comment was that if this student's church could not support him, then he could not go as a missionary.

One idea was to link him to a more wealthy church that might have had the resources to support him. Unfortunately, that was not very popular in the closing years of apartheid either. In the end, we just could not find support for him and, disillusioned with the established mission movement in South Africa, I lost touch with him.

That incident became one of the defining moments in my mission journey. Since then, I have become more and more involved in looking at ways to link global mission resources to global mission needs.

In the process, Mark 10:42-45 became a central text to me. Jesus says:

> You know that those who are regarded as rulers of the Gentiles lord it over them, and their high officials exercise authority over them. Not so with you. Instead, whoever wants to become great among you must be your servant, and whoever wants to be first must be slave of all. For even the Son of Man did not come to be served, but to serve, and to give his life as a ransom for many.

In light of this passage, I started defining mission from the perspective of sacrificial service.

God made us stewards of his resources not to hoard them for ourselves but to serve others with what he has entrusted to us. In a sense, we are given the opportunity to invite others to become joint stewards with us.

There are two main problems that we experienced in South Africa. The first was that some communities owned most of the resources and there was reluctance to share with the needy, even among Christians. The second problem is that those who want to share resources with others do not know where the most urgent and strategic needs are. It has been my concern to improve cooperation between communities and to sow vision for a network of interconnected communities of believers in Jesus, who can share their resources with one another to meet needs while advancing the gospel.

The Fruits of Interconnectedness

This vision of interconnected communities is already becoming a reality. The forces of globalization facilitate an ever-growing interdependence and interconnectedness between nations and communities, including Christian communities. There have been several results.

First, the movement of capital, people, goods, and information across national borders has increased dramatically, which has impacted business and government but also the mission and the spread of the gospel.

Second, globalization and the growing interconnectedness between communities has resulted in an increased spread of wealth. Wealth is not confined to the rich West anymore but exists now in places such as India, Russia, Asia, Latin America, and Africa. Many churches in formerly poor countries, from Guatemala and Brazil to Malaysia and Indonesia, are becoming very wealthy as these Christians give to their churches.

Within each country, however, inequality and societal division remain. This inequality is reflected in global Christianity and poses a threat to international security, with environmental degradation, violent conflict, and the trafficking of people and drugs. Many Christians are affected by these conflicts as well.

Finally, increased wealth within resource-poor nations is resulting in increased giving to social causes from within those nations. National associations of donors are being established and strengthened all over the world, with philanthropic initiatives coming from the Philippines, India, East Africa, Russia, and Latin America.

Giving to Missions in the Twenty-First Century

It is a changing world. Christian stewards are experiencing great wealth together with great poverty as population density hits its greatest mass in South and East Asia.

Meanwhile, the net income of all Christians in the world totals $18,170tn, with $390bn given by Christians to Christian causes. Seventy-eight individual countries have evangelicals whose personal income exceeds US$1bn a year. This gives an indication of the financial resource potential for missions in some of the poorer countries. To tap into this potential, we could learn a few things from our secular friends.

The European Foundation Centre (a Brussels-based non-profit association of foundations) proposes four entry points for European philanthropic organizations to engage in global philanthropy: (1) take a global view; (2) advocacy and convening; (3) investing in knowledge development, research, and innovation on global issues; and (4) collaboration. Taking seriously what the European Foundation Centre proposes, I want to suggest the following entry points for Christian individuals, groups, and churches that are involved in giving to missions in the twenty-first century.

Take a Missiological Perspective

We are God's stewards of God's resources engaged in God's mission from everywhere to everywhere. From this perspective, no individual, group, or nation can claim exclusive ownership of the resources that God has entrusted to them. Within the global body of Christ we need to carry out detailed research on mission giving in resource-poor countries and discern how we can increase this giving.

Take a Global Perspective

Christian giving initiatives need to consider the impact of globalization, global issues, and global missions. This means considering systemic and multisectoral giving that would support initiatives that touch business (for example investment in Christian-oriented businesses in poorer countries), government, education, entertainment, media, family, and religion.

Take an Informative Perspective

Christian giving needs to take place within the context of proper information on mission initiatives, context, needs, and resources. This will require research, analysis, and dissemination within the global mission community. On the basis of our findings, we can choose to support the most strategic and needed initiatives. Local information systems are preferential because they have local understanding and expertise and are well placed to be agents and knowledge resources.

Take a Strategic Perspective

If we can improve our local mission information management, then we can identify gaps, duplication, and potential synergies. These initiatives could then be supported from the outside and through more strategically targeted mission giving from within the country. Christian philanthropic institutions can take leadership roles in facilitating this more strategic side of mission engagement.

Take a Collaborative Perspective

Christian philanthropic initiatives can leverage resources and increase their impact by working collaboratively on global missions. This could be done by joining local Christian donors in supporting strategic mission initiatives on the basis of sector analysis, catalyzing new resources, or entering into existing foundational or cross-sectoral collaborative ventures.

New Opportunities

Models of such strategic resource sharing are now being developed. Here are just two examples of what I believe could be the kind of mission giving that we need in the twenty-first century: (1) The Global Mission Fund, and (2) Joint Information Management Initiative of the World Evangelical Alliance Mission Commission, the latter of which I am involved with.

The twenty-first century has become a network of increasingly interconnected communities, providing an unprecedented opportunity for the global Christian community to collaborate and share resources more strategically and effectively as it works to advance the kingdom of God.

TECHNOLOGY AND THE INTERNET IN THE CHRIST-FOLLOWING WORLD

Henry Kaestner

Trends and Opportunities for Growth in Generosity and Resource Mobilization

The Internet, much like the Gutenberg Bible, continues to revolutionize how Christ followers around the world get access to information, inspiration, and community. We at the Resource Mobilization Working Group see this trend accelerating at unprecedented rates. With the advent of the Web 2.0 sites – sites that offer fluid flow of information, targeted communication, and immediate dialogue by way of dominant platforms of Internet communication – as well as the ever-increasing access to mobile technology worldwide, the continued innovation of Internet capabilities can and will dramatically impact the Christ-following ministry in the next twenty years.

Nowhere do we see this trend having more of an impact than in resource mobilization. Christ followers at organizations such as www.Kiva.org, www.CharityWater.org, and www. GlobalFast.org are leading the way using their God-given talents to bring innovative giving tools to the world.

One of the great aspects of the Internet and technology developments as a whole, is how it democratizes content and community providing information and e-commerce applications for both the modern-day "widow" with her mite and the "rich young ruler" with his fortune.

If the current crop of resource-mobilization platforms that have come into prominence over the past several years are any indication, we know that the leading platforms of twenty years from now are likely to be an entirely different set of entities. Many of those future sites, however, are likely to be inspired by the current crop of platforms that impact resource mobilization.

Some of the following Web sites include but are not limited to:

www.Kiva.org – a platform that brings online peer-to-peer transactions to the world of microfinance.

www.CharityWater.org – a fund-raising platform for clean water, reaching the masses through a brilliant design and aesthetic, multimedia tools and live Twitter festivals from communities with new wells.

www.Durhamcares.org – a platform that highlights organizations that set outcome goals for themselves, allowing users to give directly to that charity and alerting them if/when the charity hits its goals.

www.MinistrySpotlight.org – an open platform that seeks to help Christ followers find ministries that match their passion, with an expert blog section to help users learn about effective ministry approaches.

www.GlobalFast.org – a platform (inspired by Isaiah 58) that only accepts financial donations that have been made through fasting and praying. With its "track your impact" functionality, it is particularly effective in equipping adolescents and young adults in creating a new generation of givers and in transforming the recipients of such aid as they learn its source.

www.GenerousGiving.org – less high-tech but possibly the best online resource for materials for pastors, educators, seminarians, small groups, and individuals on exploring the "Why" of giving.

www.Nationalchristian.com – one evangelical organization that is leveraging technology at a very high level in the stewardship/charitable arenas is National

Christian Foundation (NCF). All of NCF's processes harness the Web and sophisticated technologies to impact the kingdom from a financial stewardship standpoint. As a result, in just the first three and a half months of 2010, NCF has managed over 6,800 transactions totaling over $90m in contributions for thousands of givers. It also managed over 17,000 transactions totaling over $125m in grants to fund kingdom work all over the world. Virtually all of this activity is driven by the Web and other related technology, and NCF is also investing several million additional dollars in 2010 specifically to expand its method of leveraging technology for the coming decade.

www.lausanne.org/conversation – Lausanne Global Conversation (LGC) and the underlying *WorldWideOpen.org* platform are both proving to be very powerful and effective platforms and forums to share global stewardship thoughts and practices and to bring together the worldwide church.

Whether these are Web sites or other forms of innovative Web presence, we believe there are several essential ingredients that any leading resource mobilization Web site must have to be successful, and they include:

Interactive/User Contributed Content: Sites can no longer get by with a sophisticated, online business card with static data. Users need to be drawn into an experience. Blogs, forums/chat groups, and comments are all ways to make this happen.

Multimedia: MP3s, streaming video, webcams, and movies. One note: There are few places where the difference between good and great is so pronounced. A good video promoting a ministry might get a few thousand views – a great one, a few million. One needs to look no further than the videos produced for Advent Conspiracy to see what great video looks like.

Translation Services: It is essential that the global church be able to communicate readily across continents. New applications from providers such as Google offer translation services by way of API.

Social Marketing: Web sites must integrate with social marketing applications such as Facebook and Twitter.

Equip the Local Church: Aside from Scripture, the primary distribution channel for inspiration, information, and the selection of ministries to fund is the local church. Resource mobilization sites must look for ways to support this institution. Microsites and widgets are two ways to support local community and dialogue, including private discussions between pastor and church member. Individual users should also be able to access the broader content from the entire database and participate in the worldwide dialogue.

Security: Resource mobilization initiatives around the world have differing needs for security, both in terms of information readily accessible on the Web site, as well as the need for protection from outside hackers. Techniques to address these challenges might include user permissions, allowing members to access various levels of communication, and hosting their sites with certain ministry leaders that are experts in that area.

Share with Other Web Sites: This last point brings up something important that if unheeded will bring confusion, inefficiency, and leave scores of Christ followers unmotivated and resources unmobilized.

Tower of Babel

The current state of Christ following Web 2.0 sites looks a lot more like a post Tower of Babel reality than the potential of an Acts 2 environment. If you are a Christ follower in Lisbon, Portugal, and have a passion for church planting movements in Cameroon, you are not currently likely to find the Christ follower in Manchester, England, that shares that passion or, the one in Chicago that cares about Christ-Centered Economic Development there. That is because with thousands of current ministry sites, they are all likely to be going to different Web sites to get their information.

A new initiative has arisen among more than a dozen leading Web sites to share content and community among a federated, yet independent and autonomous group of Web sites. Aside from the shared development costs (why build twenty different mapping modules or Facebook applications?), this presents a great opportunity to share content and community through APIs and shared contributions to a back-end, behind-the-scenes platform administered by a not-for-profit. The governing board of such an institution is made up of ministry leaders and Christ following technologists from the for-profit sector. For more information on this initiative, please contact RMWG member, Henry Kaestner.

Furthermore, we would like to point out that the Web 2.0 sites are not the only way that technology is impacting the resource mobilization space. Some examples include the new podcast from the people at MinistrySpotlight and the digitization of the *NIV Stewardship Study Bible* and related resources from the folks at Stewardship Council.

At the Resource Mobilization Working Group, we do not believe that God needs our money to do his work. However, we believe that in marshalling his resources for his glory, we are brought closer to God. It is God who chooses to work through his people to spread his resources. Technology used in giving/resource mobilization is a ministry in and of itself with a goal to transform the lives of recipient *and* giver.

6

SETTING STANDARDS

THE OXFORD INITIATIVE: UNITING GIVERS AND RECEIVERS

Rob Martin

The Oxford Initiative

The Lausanne Standard "Oxford Initiative" is an exciting new drive to set principles and guidelines for resource senders and receivers alike and to bring about true unity and communion of purpose for kingdom work. Resourcing and receiving ministries frequently experience shifting dynamics that can lead to misunderstandings, and Oxford is an initiative to bridge the gap between the two.

How and Why It Began

The project dates back to November 2006 when a goal was set to determine how serious an issue the financial relationship between leader and donor is within missions today. The

Oxford Initiative group then carried out extensive qualitative and quantitative research to hear the unfiltered and authentic voices of leaders from all sectors and regions.

What we found was that the sharing of money in cross-cultural ministry partnerships is a substantial issue warranting serious attention. Many survey respondents said they are satisfied with their own policies and practices, but the majority mentioned troublesome issues of unity, trust, and respect between donors and implementers.

The State of Global Christian Stewardship

Traditional funding patterns have been disrupted with the rise of the global church. Money now flows with heightened expectations. Churches acting as mission senders and philanthropists are increasingly found in places where charity was already sent. It is clear that resources are being stretched. The Oxford Initiative group found that cultural readjustments of both the financial sender and receiver alike are needed.

Leaders from various sectors of the church, including Western funders and senior non-Western members of the Lausanne movement, agreed with our findings. They call for a process to bring some semblance of balance and order to the sometimes acrimonious and often confusing interactions between resources and missions.

The Problems We Must Face

Many of the issues encountered when looking at problems between ministries and funders have to do with competition for resources. Ministries often exaggerate numbers to give a good report, and donors can be at fault with the questions they ask. There is also a lot of hurt and some animosity to Western donors, so determining whose words are the truth can be very difficult.

A Need for Accountability

We need a framework of open dialogue that allows people to feel they have permission to tell the truth. Accountability takes work but should not be avoided. The word *accountability* can be misappropriated to allow parties to act in a heavy-handed way or allow for a lack of trust. However, it is scriptural (2 Cor. 8:20) and wisdom is impossible without it. For example, good accountability prevents the misuse of funds and fosters closer relationships.

True accountability is about truth and honesty, partnership and collaboration. Giving one another the permission to tell the truth can be difficult, but it is always a learning process. Receiving ministries need to find out what donors are looking for, as much as resource providers need to know what is really happening on the ground.

A Need for Cooperation

The Oxford Initiative aims to establish Lausanne standards that will enable donors and receivers to work more closely together. Ultimately, our goal is to bring more integrity to the process and to encourage more efficient giving.

On a practical note, the Oxford Initiative hopes to create a set of protocols to connect funders with implementers and bring a common understanding of words such as *outcomes*, *proposals*, and *reports*. It will also deal with cross-cultural issues and challenges when making grants, such as reporting, accountability, and faithfulness to the grant parameters.

Above all, the Oxford Initiative will allow parties to communicate more freely with each other in truth and honesty, while being more accountable to each other and working in unity for the good of the kingdom.

FINDING NEW MODELS OF FUNDING

Phill Butler

Setting Standards Means Seeking Out Best Practices

The vision of the Oxford Initiative is that Christians will begin to proactively find, assess, and replicate currently effective, but largely undiscovered, funding models that can help to power world evangelization.

As the church becomes global, new models for funding world evangelization and holistic ministry are essential. Old funding models rooted in traditional regional relationships are inadequate and do not capitalize on the remarkably creative alternative options that exist. In some cases, they are actually counterproductive to the growth of the non-Western church's contribution, as well as the Western church's role.

Historically, modern missions initiatives have been funded by a model of church-based support in the form of denominational support, individual church support, and support by individuals from within local churches. The Oxford Initiative seeks to increase emphasis in leadership development among non-Western leaders on the themes of money and stewardship, and on creative alternatives for funding the work of God.

Our Action Plan Toward More Effective Global Stewardship

We would like to see a significant increase in funding for kingdom purposes, and believe this can be achieved by pursuing a three-pronged strategy:

First, make a highly focused, intentional effort to increase awareness and kingdom-based education within the Western church around the themes of money and stewardship. This is covered in the first three chapters of this book – looking at the theology of holistic stewardship, compelling case studies, and the heart behind giving.

Second, identify, promote, and encourage income-generating models and projects specifically established and maintained for a funding purpose. Some models will be well established but not widely adopted; others will be born out of innovation rooted in opportunities presented in each local context. Specifically, the Oxford Initiative envisions all, or a predetermined percentage of income over expenses being channeled directly to the kingdom project. This is in contrast to income first going through the pocket of the individual believers and then through the administrative/decision-making process of the local church or denomination.

We believe the Lausanne movement, with its regional structures, specialized working groups, communications infrastructure, and wider spheres of influence can have a significant impact in both stewardship education and innovation of models for giving.

We are already seeing a number of effective initiatives as illustrated in chapter 2, and we know there is already a high level of innovation and successful business networking in Latin American countries, Nigeria, South Africa, India, Indonesia, Philippines, Hong Kong/China, Korea, and elsewhere.

As we develop standards for finding and encouraging innovative funding models, the Oxford Initiative aims to establish primary regional partners where research and development can be based and where there is reasonable likelihood that there can be ongoing education, training, encouragement, and support for replication. These regional bases can also serve as an accountability pipeline for kingdom venture capital to flow into later on, as a result, of the research and development project.

As part of the standards process, we will also seek to develop a database of contacts and develop a format to describe these models that will allow an accessible, searchable database to be integrated into or function alongside of the contact database. This will enable us to quickly identify projects and models that warrant a closer look. These models will be marked out by their simplicity, demonstrated performance, ability to be replicated or scaled up, the resources that are required (financial, intellectual, technical, capital), or by their relevance to non-Western involvement and application.

Hopes and Dreams

Our hope for this initiative is to encourage non-Western leaders in the funding/development sectors to adopt new funding models that are strong, sustainable alternatives to the older, often dependency-producing models.

Our aim is to assist with new and sustainable models of funding that engage the global church in true partnership. We trust that, in undertaking these initiatives, there is a powerful potential for renewal within the Western church and beyond.

CHRIST-CENTERED ECONOMIC DEVELOPMENT

Henry Kaestner

What Is CCED?

The Christ-Centered Economic Development Initiative (CCED) is a Christian mission group that uses economic development as the primary vehicle to help serve the physical needs of the poor. With a constant goal of sharing the gospel in a more open and collaborative context, the CCED fosters sustainability and dignity, rather than dependency.

The CCED initiative has shown tremendous promise in more than a decade of application throughout the world of missions. It has proven successful in addressing the physical needs of those in developing countries and has been a key agent in the spread of the gospel, particularly when used in collaboration with the local church.

Unfortunately, despite its efficacy CCED has yet to receive widespread support among Christian donors, compared to more traditional, noneconomic focused missions work such as mercy ministry initiatives for schools, hospitals, orphan care, and food relief. Herein lies the tension of the need to fund such crucial systemic efforts in addition to tending to the most visible, immediate, and felt needs. For this reason, an increasing number of Christians are excited about bringing CCED into the mainstream. These people recognize that while the CCED industry and its practitioners have driven solid progress, there is still much work to be done before CCED can scale its funding and operations.

The Future Strategy of CCED

The work ahead includes studying the impact of CCED in the field, both in terms of spiritual and secular outcomes, and solidifying, formalizing, and improving each organization's internal and external operations. CCED proponents need to develop a marketing plan that will be relevant and effective at generating widespread interest and funding from the community, both Christian and secular, local and international. It also needs to have a definition specifying the Christ-centered principles that make it effective in spreading the gospel and serving the poor. This definition will defend against the significant temptations that may cause a Christ-centered organization to stray from their Christian principles, in order to achieve funding and organizational growth.

Standardizing CCED Activity

Our aim in seeking to develop standards for CCED is to see the initiative reach greater adoption, and ultimately help CCED practitioners and participants to extend the kingdom of God.

As mentioned, the standards process will aim to provide a generally acknowledged definition of CCED, with shared agreement on its "nonnegotiable" mission and applications. It will endeavor to lay out a set of clear principles and values that help guide practitioners in application and donors in providing support.

Other benefits of standardizing on CCED include studying the impact of spreading the gospel among the communities in which CCED operates; and providing practitioners with research that will help them understand their recipient and donor target markets. It will provide a framework for the independent review and audit of the Christ-centered aspects of CCED work (particularly in the field among case workers/ service providers) in a way that serves the missions of the organizations as well as the concerns of donors.

Groundwork for Action

As a starting point, the RMWG would like to suggest the following set of Christ-centered principles and values to be agreed upon by all parties who take part in the CCED initiative, and we invite dialogue on the points raised.

All CCED organizations hereby agree:

- That the highest goal and aim is to make disciples of Christ – to teach one to "Love the Lord your God with all your heart, soul, and mind."

- That Christ-Centered Economic Development must also respond to the second command "to love your neighbor (with the broader definition as applied in the Parable of the Good Samaritan) as yourself," as well as the call in Matthew 25:40 to take care of the "least of these."

- To work in conjunction with the local church wherever possible. CCED organizations are not a replacement for, but a collaborative partner of, the local church.

- That these endeavors are for the greater glory of God and not of their organizations.
- To hire only Christian caseworkers who have been well vetted by local churches, have earned the right to share the gospel and/or can point CCED recipients in the direction of the local church.
- That caseworkers aim for excellence in providing physical assistance for their clients; modeling the life of Christ; and being a part of the local church and pointing others to the local church.
- To submit themselves to external audit and review of an independent agency that ensures compliance with CCED principles.
- To endeavor to build and manage their organizations in a highly professional and measurable way.

We recognize that some providers may be wary of subjecting their organizations to external review, but our hope is that they will understand that this will be for the greater good of their missions. It will also allow them to be much more effective at raising money.

Sustaining Dignity, Not Dependency

Some reflections on CCED are that the initiative has the ability to create a culture of dignity rather than dependency; it does not take the place of medical missions, orphanages, schools, and the like, but with modest economic gains it can make those institutions, and the positive change they drive, more sustainable. Finally, CCED has the potential to make the church stronger by helping the laypeople of the church to bless the community.

7

UNITY: PRACTICING
RELATIONAL STEWARDSHIP

RELATIONAL STEWARDSHIP: A STUDY

Norris Hill

Community in Scripture

Throughout Scripture, God is constantly calling his people into community: Jesus gathered disciples together, and in Acts the apostles lived and gave to one another selflessly as the first churches were formed. While Christ followers may have experienced seasons of seclusion and prayer, God always drew them back into deep relationship with other believers.

God by nature is communal. Scripture unfolds the mystery of the Holy Trinity and we see God in relationship with himself: Father, Son and Holy Spirit. Genesis 1:26 speaks of God in the plural: "Let us make man in our image, in our likeness."

John 1 says, "In the beginning was the Word, and the Word was with God, and the Word was God." This is the mystery of the triune Godhead: one God, in community with himself.

Upon salvation, believers are brought into this relationship. We go boldly before the Father's throne of grace. Christ is in us, we are in him and the Holy Spirit moves our hearts. As we walk in the reality of our identity in Christ we are embodiments of him on earth. Community, therefore, is a fuller representation of God's character. When God calls his people together, they quite literally form the body of Christ, a people with endless potential in him.

Relational Stewardship

Relational stewardship springs from Christ's words in John 13:34-35, "A new commandment I give to you, that you love one another, even as I have loved you, that you also love one another." If we are to love one another as Christ loved us, this means through relationship. It is important, however, to realize that there is no power in relationship in and of itself. It is the object of our relationship that is important. The only true power for life and transformation is Christ. If relationship is not Christ-breathed, then it is an exercise of the flesh.

Therefore, to be a good steward is to let yourself be loved in a relationship with Christ and to let others be loved by Christ through your continued relationship with them. This is relational stewardship: a pursuit of God's unique vision and call on an individual's life through consistent Christ-centered relationship.

Building the Kingdom to Share God's Truth

It is tempting for Christ followers to become obsessed with kingdom work. That is to say, we subtly buy into the idea that we are solely responsible for the continued existence of God's project on this earth. However, this is wrong; there is nothing fragile about God, Christ, or his truth. It is the immutable fact of all existence. It is the flame that can never be extinguished.

Practicing relational stewardship, therefore, is not using intimate relationship to coddle the embers of God's truth. It is using it as a platform to wave his torch in the face of life's storms. It is a beacon to those lost in the darkness. The kingdom of God is in no danger of disappearing, but as Christ followers, we fight a constant battle to keep our eyes on the truth.

A Culture of Spiritual Responsibility

Just as Christ poured himself into the lives of the disciples, we are to pour our lives into each other. Just as he told the twelve to journey together, we are to gather together. Christ does leave the ninety-nine to pursue the one lost sheep, but he always brings the one back to the flock.

We were created to know him along side one another. When we do this, we are no longer living as spiritual islands but as part of a larger body. Relational stewardship becomes the modus operandi and a culture of spiritual responsibility is formed.

A culture of spiritual responsibility exists when God raises up consistent generations with a deep understanding and commitment to the disciplines of grace and living out of his power. This is where we learn that we do not tend the fires of the gospel but that they tend to us.

People are born into a tragic paradox: We were created to live by Christ's life, yet, in our sin, we have been separated from him. In the same way that those living in the blackness of the world could not conceive of something as close and bright as fire, our hearts and minds could never concoct the life and light of Christ.

Christ has given us the gift of himself and of one another. By his power, we journey toward him together. Here he fashions the tools by which he will rebuild our ruined cities. Here his people can dwell for generations. All we must do is use what he has freely given.

Releasing God's Gifts and Unity

Terry Douglass

A desire for unity in the body of Christ drives the work of the Lausanne movement. With the goal to accelerate the whole church in taking the whole gospel to the whole world, unity is essential.

The Situation Today

The global church has over $18 trillion in annual personal income and untold trillions in assets. Yet, less than 2.5 percent, around $390 billion, is given to Christian causes each year. Less than 0.1 percent, or $15bn, is given to foreign missions. There are currently around 1.8bn unevangelized people living in the world. At the current rate of Christian giving and population growth it is projected that by 2025 there will be 2.2bn – missions are going backward! We urgently need a concerted effort to mobilize financial resources for world evangelization, and the only way we are going to do this is to work together in unity.

The Resource Mobilization Working Group

The Resource Mobilization Working Group (RMWG) was initiated under the Lausanne Committee for World Evangelization (LCWE) to provide focused leadership, godly collaboration, and to develop a strategy to significantly discover, develop, and mobilize all of God's global material and financial resources. In a nutshell, the vision of the RMWG is "to create a global culture of spiritual responsibility and generosity."

Just imagine if we, as a movement, could affect the existing giving pattern by raising the current 2.5 percent of giving to a 10 percent threshold. It would result in an additional $1.3 trillion in financial resourcing of global evangelization!

We pray that the Lausanne Cape Town 2010 conference will establish a new global paradigm for both unity and kingdom stewardship. Our desire is to see the whole church taking the whole gospel to the whole world, and whole-church biblical stewardship coming together into a holistic union.

Ephesians 4:1-16: Unity in the Body of Christ

A key passage on which to base our hope and practice is Ephesians 4:1-16:

> As a prisoner for the Lord, then, I urge you to live a life worthy of the calling you have received. Be completely humble and gentle; be patient, bearing with one another in love. Make every effort to keep the unity of the Spirit through the bond of peace. There is one body and one Spirit – just as you were called to one hope when you were called – one Lord, one faith, one baptism; one God and Father of all, who is over all and through all and in all.
>
> But to each one of us grace has been given as Christ apportioned it. This is why it says: "When he ascended on high, he led captives in his train and gave gifts to men."
>
> (What does "he ascended" mean except that he also descended to the lower, earthly regions? He who descended is the very one who ascended higher than all the heavens, in order to fill the whole universe.) It was he who gave some to be apostles, some to be prophets, some to be evangelists, and some to be pastors and teachers, to prepare God's people for works of service, so that the body of Christ may be built up until we all reach unity in the faith and in the knowledge of the

Son of God and become mature, attaining to the whole measure of the fullness of Christ.

Then we will no longer be infants, tossed back and forth by the waves, and blown here and there by every wind of teaching and by the cunning and craftiness of men in their deceitful scheming. Instead, speaking the truth in love, we will in all things grow up into him who is the Head, that is, Christ. From him the whole body, joined and held together by every supporting ligament, grows and builds itself up in love, as each part does its work.

SUSTAINABLE GIVING THROUGH COLLABORATIVE PARTNERSHIPS

Henry Kaestner

Toward Collaboration

In January 2009, a dozen leaders of Christ-centered mercy ministries along with several business leaders got together in Raleigh, North Carolina, for two days of encouragement and collaboration. They discussed how they might work together more effectively in the common pursuit of extending the kingdom of God and meeting the needs of the poor in a transformative and sustainable way.

It became clear from the meeting that cooperation between business and ministry was a familiar concept and an idea that had merit but that it had not yet been deployed in a real and effective way. This was due to a host of logistical issues and an admitted overarching focus on each organization's own separate mission and fund-raising needs. Upon reflection, this internal focus came at the unintentional expense of the populations that they served.

Toward Effective and Sustainable Service

The leaders realized that a more holistic ministry approach would be more effective in attending to the complete needs of the populations they served. Such an approach could incorporate ministries such as – but not limited to – church planting, economic development, microfinance institutions (MFI), medical clinics, clean water, youth discipleship, schools, and leadership training.

For example, if there is an organization focused on orphan care in location "X," but there is no economic development in place to support these children, as they become adults, then the transformation cannot be sustained. In the same way, it was agreed that the gospel must be a cornerstone of any true transformation within a community.

In the weeks and months that have passed since this meeting, several of us have met together regularly to discuss what the potential might be for collaboration among leading providers of mercy ministries in a deployment abroad of partnered organizations that together provide a holistic ministry program for those being served. It is our hope that we have provided enough of a background on the opportunity for collaboration to now get input from other influential leaders in Christ-Centered Mercy Ministries.

Laying the Groundwork

In an effort to increase the effectiveness of giving and thereby change the way that people think about giving, we present the following set of hypotheses:

1. As capital is used more efficiently to help the poor, givers should come to expect real, measurable results from their gifts. As these measurable results are proven and studied, givers will be more inclined to continue and/or increase their giving as they better understand the impact of their investments.

2. By linking together independent agencies in a collaborative format, we can significantly increase the outcomes and results. A key differentiator for the proposed collaborative model is that the involved agencies remain independent so as to preserve their own agility and creativity, as opposed to a model where all the ministries are under a formalized collective structure.

3. The proposed collaboration and the accountability it brings will result in significant increases in metrics from their collective efforts. Collaboration will also present opportunities for savings in program expenses.

4. The combination of increased metrics and decreased expenses will be a catalyst for further growth in these collaborative efforts and will attract more funding as the "return" from investment in these organizations becomes clearer and more tangible.

5. Ultimately, we hope that this approach will get twice the outcome with half the investment, and that, once proven, studied, and presented, it might lead to ten times the giving as it will be able to more effectively tap into both Christian and secular sources.

6. Secular funding sources will be drawn to these initiatives for pragmatic reasons such as measurable increases in employment, decreases in infant mortality, and other effects that we hope these collaborations will drive in the field.

We would love to see these six hypotheses in effect on a larger scale, which could lead to the following results:

It would foster collaboration among independent, autonomous and complementary Christ-centered mercy ministries, for which it would provide funding. It would lead to the research and study of collaborative practices among international aid organizations in both a secular and Christ-centered environment.

We would gain research and study outcomes and metrics in both spiritual (church attendance, confessions of faith) and secular (infant mortality, employment) terms.

A larger collaborative partnership would communicate its findings, as one body, to potential donors in a fashion that would hold up to rigorous academic scrutiny and due diligence of potential donors.

It would create an organization that would seek to provide ongoing assistance (research, consulting, etc.) to collaborative Christ-centered mercy ministries.

Finally, it will have the ability to sponsor conferences and events that would serve to encourage, inspire, educate and provide recreation and rest for these ministries.

Getting Practical

In order to test out the hypotheses detailed above, the RMWG intends to identify up to five pilots where there are independent agencies that would be willing to work together toward a holistic approach of transforming a community. We will invest in these five control groups and keep, analyze, and regularly communicate meticulous data on how it works and why.

We will look for the following four attributes in our deployments:

1. Leadership from indigenous citizens is preferable; wherever possible, initiatives on the ground should be led by in-country citizens. Where this is not possible, multiple successor candidates should be identified and nurtured.

2. We will aim for demand-driven solutions with feedback loops – in other words, solutions where those being assisted vote with their participation, money, and so on.

3. The attribute we will look for is church-centered deployments, because all initiatives are to support, not supplant the local church.

4. We will plan sustainable projects with a minimum of investment from the outside to seek economic growth and sustainability at two different levels:

The first level is community initiatives that fund themselves, though we recognize that the 100 percent level will be difficult with just MFI. Orphanages, youth discipleship, and so forth, will require significant funding. Some will be at least partially able to support themselves, for example, medical clinics, schools, and clean water projects. Overall, sustainability should be a key goal and while a magic number – say 80 percent sustainability – might not be appropriate, constant vigilance toward the goal of sustainability is essential.

The second level of sustainable projects is outside funding from within the country, rather than from the Western world. As much of a funding requirement as possible should come from other sources within the country. For example, we could encourage Mumbai Christians to support our community initiative outside of Pune, rather than relying solely on a church just outside of Chicago.

On a final note, it should be mentioned that all organizations will need to adhere to a biblically sound, Spirit-led, gospel-centric creed.

Conclusion

Brett Elder
Stephen Grabill

As the body of Christ, the church, expands over the globe, sustaining effective, relational stewardship becomes a difficult task, requiring thought and reflection, analysis and innovation, and, most essentially, collaboration across great distances. For this reason, the focus of Cape Town 2010 has been the great need for untiy – unity in our understanding of stewardship, in our plans of action, and collaborative unity as we carry out these plans.

This focus on unity has been apparent in the seven chapters of these kingdom stewardship papers, but the variety of authors and essays included has given us a wider perspective and an obvious sense of the most important and urgent issues in resource mobilization. These watershed issues include the problem of weakening generosity between giver and receiver, which, in turn, reflect weakening economic and relational realities, the untapped potential of modern technology, the need for greater innovation within giving models, and a need for greater accountability.

The first issue mentioned by multiple authors is also the most straightforward and easy to measure – a drop in financial giving. Terry Douglass cites that less than 2.5 percent of personal income within the Christian church goes to Christian causes each year. Sas Conradie puts a face on these statistics, illustrating that a drop in contributions goes together with mission projects halted for lack of funds. A drop in giving also marks a dysfunction in the hearts of Christ followers. As Paul Schultheis points out in the strongholds chapter, the modern impulse to hoard our savings is the opposite of a God-inspired desire to give.

There is also agreement on the need for a transition from old models of giving to newer, more efficient models that make use of the Internet and other modern advancements. Henry Kaestner compares the current presence of Web-based Christian charity to the Tower of Babel, a teetering effort that is neither united nor well-focused. Many of our authors emphasize the need to actively seek out and determine the most effective models for Christian stewardship that best utilize the expertise of local leaders and organizations. The consensus is there; what is needed next is concerted effort and sufficient resources.

Another key word that our authors used with frequency throughout this book is accountability. Well-meaning Christian leaders can set out to further the kingdom of God, forming partnerships, giving generously, intelligently, and strategically, but responsible stewards must follow through on their efforts, and, for this, open and honest dialogue is essential.

Accountability, as well as the drive to innovate and the impulse to give, begins in the heart. The Christian sense of identity as a steward of God comes from an understanding of God's grace and the love he poured out to us in Jesus Christ. As Norris Hill writes in the chapter on relational stewardship, it is our relationship with Christ that motivates our love for others. It is through this relational stewardship that his love is shared among all peoples. When we find ourselves in the midst of such a relationship, we cannot be more eager to become better stewards because we understand, as Hill writes, "We do not tend the fires of the gospel, but that they tend to us." We are all one in the church, even on the international level. How could we not desire to become more effective stewards of the body of Christ?

The Lausanne movement is the expression of this shared desire to better tend the kingdom of God. So, to this end, let us work toward greater global unity, strategic collaboration, and effective stewardship of our world, motivated by a shared understanding of Christ's love for us all.

CONTRIBUTORS

PHILL BUTLER started his professional career as an international broadcast journalist, which included many years with *ABC News*. He then moved on to broadcast management and consulting. Following his career in broadcasting over the last thirty years, first as head of Intercristo, then Interdev, he has worked in over seventy countries. He has written extensively in the field of communications, current affairs and missions, and is the author of the recently published *Well Connected: Releasing Power, Restoring Hope Through Kingdom Partnerships* (World Vision/Authentic Media, 2006). He now heads VisionSynergy, a ministry focused on international ministry network development. He is married to Marni Muir Butler, has two daughters and three grandchildren, and lives in Seattle, Washington. He is a scuba diver, sailor, photographer, and former Pacific Coast road racing champion.

DR. SAS CONRADIE, a South African by birth, is currently living in the United Kingdom where he is head of the Global Mission Fund (a mission grants ministry of the Church Mission Society and the World Evangelical Alliance Mission Commission) and coordinator of the Lausanne movement/ World Evangelical Alliance related Resource Mobilization Working Group. Sas has been involved in various mission initiatives since his commitment to become a disciple of Christ in 1982. This involvement includes mobilizing South African students to engage in world evangelization from the mid 1980s to 1990s, executive director of the South African National Initiative for Reconciliation, Christian community development initiatives, outreach to Muslims as missionary to Ukraine, and leadership positions in a number of mission initiatives. An ordained minister in the Dutch Reformed Church, Sas received a DD in missiology from the University of Pretoria in 1996 and has held different academic positions. A fervent networker, Sas served as chairman of the Joint Information Management Initiative (a taskforce of the World Evangelical Alliance Mission Commission) from 2006-2010.

DR. TERRY DOUGLASS is currently serving as a special advisor to the executive chairman of the Lausanne Committee for World Evangelization (LCWE) and is a member of the LCWE Resource Mobilization Working Group. He is also president of ProVision Healthcare, LLC (www.pvhealthcare. com) and ProVision Trust, Inc., and chairman of the board of ProVision Foundation, Inc. (www.provisionfoundation.org).

Terry served as the chairman of the board of CTI Molecular Imaging, Inc., a public company that specialized in the development, production, and distribution of products and services for the medical diagnostic imaging market from 1983 to 2005 when it was acquired by Siemens. He also served as president and CEO of CTI Molecular Imaging from its formation in 1983 until 2003. During this tenure, he played an integral role in the development and commercialization of PET (positron emission technology) technology and development globally as well as PET cyclotron technology, which technologies now play a significant role in proton therapy. He was also instrumental in the development of Medicare reimbursement for PET services.

He graduated with B.S., M.S., and Ph.D. degrees in electrical engineering from the University of Tennessee. He has been married for forty-six years to Rosann Bobbitt Douglass, and they have three married children and ten grandchildren.

BRETT ELDER is executive director of the Stewardship Council, a leading producer of resources in holistic stewardship education. Brett provided the vision and executive editorial oversight for Zondervan's recently released *NIV Stewardship Study Bible*, Stewardship Council's flagship resource. Brett has invested the last decade teaching biblical stewardship and the grace of giving to leaders throughout the developing world through the ministry of International Steward – an organization he helped launch in 2000.

DR. DION FORSTER is a consultant and chaplain to the Power Group of Companies as well as the Global Day of Prayer and Unashamedly Ethical movements. Dion serves as a Christian minister in the corporate sector. He holds a doctorate in theology and science and teaches at various South African universities. Dion Forster and Graham Power are the authors of *Transform Your Work Life: Turn Your Ordinary Day into an Extraordinary Calling* (Struik Christian Books, 2010).

RAM GIDOOMAL CBE came to Britain from East Africa as a refugee in 1967. He is an entrepreneur and former United Kingdom Group chief executive of the Inlaks Group, a multinational business with seven thousand employees. He is chairman of Winning Communications Partnership, South Asian

Concern, Citylife (Industrial and Provident Society) Ltd., a board member of the International Justice Mission, an external member of the Audit and Risk Committee of the UK Equalities and Human Rights Commission, a council member of the United Kingdom Evangelical Alliance, and chairman of the steering group of the South Asian Forum of the UKEA.

Ram was founding chairman of the Christmas Cracker charity, which has given thousands of young people direct entrepreneurial experience and has raised over £5 million for projects in developing countries. He was the leader of the Christian Peoples Alliance and ran as their candidate for London Mayor and Assembly in 2000 and 2004 gaining just under 100,000 votes in each election.

He is a motivational public speaker, frequent media commentator, and the author of several books including *The UK Maharajahs* and *The British and How to Deal with Them: Doing Business with Britain's Ethnic Communities*. He is a governor of King's College School in Wimbledon, and he serves as chairman of the Lausanne Resource Mobilization Working Group and is deputy chairman of the Lausanne International Board of Directors.

Ram is married to Sunita and has three children and two grandchildren.

DR. STEPHEN GRABILL serves as senior research scholar in theology at Acton Institute, a Grand Rapids, Michigan-based think tank that integrates Christian worldview with economics for leaders in the church, academy, and business sectors. He is editor emeritus of the *Journal of Markets & Morality*, as well as general editor of the *NIV Stewardship Study Bible*, an Evangelical Christian Publishers Association (ECPA) 2010 award-contending resource, and a founding board member of Stewardship Council, the producer of the study Bible and a leader in the development and delivery of stewardship resources. He graduated from Calvin Theological Seminary with a doctorate in systematic theology, after having spent more than a decade exploring the insights of the Reformed tradition on ethics, politics, and culture. He is author of *Rediscovering the Natural Law in Reformed Theological Ethics* (Eerdmans, 2006) and editor of *Sourcebook in Late-Scholastic Monetary Theory* (Lexington, 2007).

NORRIS HILL is married to Melissa, and they have four children and live in Knoxville, Tennessee. Norris served in the United States Marine Corps, attended the University of Tennessee, spent ten years on staff with Young Life, and now works with his family foundation (ProVision).

KENT HUMPHREYS has been a business leader for over forty years. While owning and operating a nationwide general merchandise distribution business, he worked with the nation's largest retailers. Since selling the family business in 1997, Kent continues to be involved in real estate, private equities, and a medical distribution business. From 2002 through 2007, he was president of Fellowship of Companies for Christ International, an organization that equips and encourages Christian business owners who desire to use their companies as a platform for ministry. Kent now serves them as a worldwide ambassador for FCCI (Christ@Work).

For many years, Kent has spent much of his time ministering to business leaders, pastors, and students across the country through speaking, writing, and mentoring. He and his wife Davidene have written a number of books including *Show and Then Tell, Shepherding Horses (vols. 1 and 2), Christ@Work: Opening Doors*, and *Christ@Work: In Your Transition*. Kent and Davidene have three children and eight grandchildren, and they make their home in Oklahoma City.

HENRY KAESTNER is the founder of Resource Mobilization Ministries, a ministry focused on the "where" of giving with three distinct ministry focuses: DurhamCares.org, a local organization focused on ministry to citizens of his hometown as they "love their neighbor," the Kingdom Technology Foundation, focused on providing technology assistance to excellent ministries, and MinistrySpotlight.org, which is focused on helping Christ followers find ministries that match their passions and learn from international ministry leaders through blogs and podcasts.

Henry is also the executive chairman of Bandwidth.com, a U.S. provider of telecommunications services, a company that he cofounded with his business and ministry partner, David Morken. Henry is married and lives with his wife, Kimberley, and their three sons in Durham, North Carolina.

ROB MARTIN is partner with the First Fruit Institute serving ministries and colleague foundations as a coach on varied fund-raising, grant making, and organizational issues. He also serves with the Lausanne Committee for World Evangelization as senior associate for global philanthropy, as a seminar leader on fund-raising and leadership for missions with the Overseas Ministry Study Center, as a faculty member of the World Evangelical Alliance Leadership Institute, and as the co-executive director of the Oxford Standards Initiative.

ARIF MOHAMED is a freelance writer and editor who trained as a journalist in the United Kingdom in the early 1990s. While working as a daily news reporter in London, he interviewed people such as Bill Gates and Michael Dell. Arif gave his life to Jesus having come from a Muslim background. He specializes in magazine feature writing, covering business and technology issues, the voluntary sector, and current affairs and lifestyle matters. Arif has written for a range of businesses, IT, and consumer titles including *The Times*, *Accountancy Age*,

CIO, Computer Weekly, and *IoD Director Magazine,* and for corporate clients including Microsoft, Hewlett Packard, and BlackBerry.

GRAHAM POWER is the founder and board chairman of the Power Group of Companies. The Power Group is the largest privately owned highway construction, property development, and civil engineering company in South Africa. In 2001, Graham Power was the visionary leader for a gathering in Cape Town that saw forty-five thousand Christians fill Newlands Stadium to pray for the needs of the nation. Today this movement has become a global movement that operates in every country across the earth – the Global Day of Prayer. Graham is also the founder of the Unashamedly Ethical campaign that challenges persons to a lifestyle of values, ethics, and clean living.

PAUL SCHULTHEIS graduated in 1966 with a degree in management science from California State University in Los Angeles and in 1971 with an M.B.A. from Pepperdine University. In addition, Paul has taken numerous graduate and management courses at California State University in Los Angeles, Caltech Industrial Relations Institute, and the University of Michigan. He has taught management courses at Caltech Industrial Relations Institute and Pepperdine University Graduate School of Business.

Prior to entering the real estate field, Paul spent ten years in the electric utility industry, working in various corporate staff positions for the Southern California Edison Company. His final position with this firm was that of manager of corporate planning, in which he gained considerable experience in long-range planning, budgeting, and economic forecasting.

From 1976 to 2004, Paul devoted himself full-time to real estate, specializing in the acquisition, syndication, development and sale of income property and managing venture capital invested by both individuals and institutions. He is currently the CEO of Real Property Investment Services, Inc., as well as managing partner of Strategic Resource Group, a nonprofit organization that he founded in 2000. He has acted as general partner on numerous real estate projects, and has syndicated residential, commercial, and medical office projects in Southern California and Arizona.

JOHN C. VAN DRUNEN is an attorney and a certified public accountant with a J.D. from Regent University School of Law and graduated *magna cum laude* with an accounting degree from Anderson University's Falls School of Business. He has devoted much of his time to working in tax-exempt tax policy and other nonprofit related matters. He currently serves as in-house legal counsel and director of compliance for the Evangelical Council for Financial Accountability, Washington, D.C.

John and his wife, Lauren, both work with Christian ministries and have traveled abroad working with ministries to help spread the gospel. He is blessed to be able to assist ministries and pastors on technical tax and nonprofit matters through his writing and speaking.

Christian's **⬥ LIBRARY PRESS**

Founded in 1979 by Gerard Berghoef and Lester DeKoster, **CHRISTIAN'S LIBRARY PRESS** has been committed to publishing influential texts on church leadership, the vocation of work, and stewardship for more than thirty years. During that time Berghoef and DeKoster wrote significant works including *The Deacons Handbook*, *The Elders Handbook*, and *God's Yardstick*, which still are in demand today. After the passing of Lester DeKoster in 2009, the imprint is now administered by the Acton Institute for the Study of Religion & Liberty. For more information about Christian's Library Press, visit www.clpress.com.

THE **R**ESOURCE **M**OBILIZATION **W**ORKING **G**ROUP **(RMWG)** was initiated under the Lausanne Committee for World Evangelization (LCWE) to provide vision for a global culture of generosity and effective stewardship of God's resources to support world evangelization. The mission of the **RMWG** is to enable the discovery, development, and deployment of God's resources for world evangelization by catalyzing Global Generosity Networks in the twelve Lausanne regions.